Wim J. van Heuvel **Structuralism in**

Dutch architecture

Uitgeverij 010 Publishers, Rotterdam 1992

This publication has been made possible by a grant of the Dutch Ministry of Welfare,
Health and Culture Affairs
© 1992 Wim J. van Heuvel, Uitgeverij 010 Publishers

Book design: Piet Gerards and Marc Vleugels, Heerlen
Translation: Michael O'Loughlin, Amsterdam
Lithography: Tripiti, Rotterdam
Printing: de Bussy Ellerman Harms, Amsterdam
CIP Koninklijke Bibliotheek, Den Haag
ISBN 90 6450 152 1

Contents

Structuralism in Dutch architecture

Burgerweeshuis, Amsterdam, 1960. Aldo van Eyck

The building of the Burgerweeshuis (Orphanage) in Amsterdam around 1960 was a new milestone in European architecture. Its effect turned out to be comparable to that of Berlage's Beurs in Amsterdam and the Zonnestraal sanatorium in Hilversum by Duiker and Bijvoet. In the architecture of the Burgerweeshuis, a new architectural style made its entrance with an unexpected wealth of spatial transitions between interiors and the immediate surroundings around the building; as well as this, a strong social commitment was to be seen in the purpose of the complex. These qualities made the Burgerweeshuis the first built manifesto of the basic principles of a new editorial group of the journal Forum, which started in 1960 and was quickly known as the **Forum group**. Among its most inspiring and passionate spokesmen were Aldo van Eyck, Herman Hertzberger and Jaap Bakema. They had a great influence on a generation of young architects who interpreted the Burgerweeshuis in their own work in all kinds of ways. It led to a movement in Dutch architecture which has become known as **structuralism**. It was a reaction to post-war functionalism in Dutch architecture, with the achievement of the early decades of twentieth century architecture being studied once again.

Innovations commence

The work of the architect H.P. Berlage (1856–1934) occupies a central place within Dutch architecture in the breaking away from the nineteenth century neo-styles. For the competition for a new exchange building for Amsterdam in 1883, Berlage and his older partner Th. Sanders entered a design, in the style of the Dutch Renaissance which Hendrick de Keyser had already used for the very first Amsterdam exchange, which by then had already been demolished and replaced by a design by Jan D. Zocher jr. It was the period of the neo-styles; the design by the Viennese architect Otto Wagner for the Amsterdam competition showed a neo-classical exchange building with a monumental portico which was immediately rejected by the jury. Berlage's design was greatly altered at the end of the 1880s. There was a rupture with historicizing architecture, also within Berlage's own work. The sketches were then only exhibited in public after it had been put out to tender. The lucidly designed building volume had what were for that time remarkably level walls in which works of art were included at various points. This modern design was also to be found inside the building, where large-scale use was made of clean masonry. At points where there is extra pressure the brickwork is supplemented by stone. The steel trusses overhead are left visible in the exchange halls. Berlage was to further develop, in the course of a sizable oeuvre, the new trail he had blazed with his Beurs. He was to constantly add innovations in the architecture and the use of materials. An interesting example of this is the head office of 'De Nederlanden van 1845', which was designed in 1921–1922 and built between 1924 and 1927. In the exterior, Berlage gave clear expression to the use of a concrete skeleton. The skeleton which remains visible, is filled in with brickwork and steel windows. The powerful expressiveness of the elevations is derived from the layout of the floor plans with striking entrances and stairways. Noticeable is the reduction of the bays of the ground floor to the halved bays with two windows on the first floor. The console-like projection of the first floor is designed in a logical manner on the basis of the construction in reinforced concrete. Shortly before his death Berlage designed the second floor of the building, which was built in 1954 under the direction of the architect W.M. Dudok.

Reactions to Berlage's work

In his own country, Berlage's work was to inspire strongly divergent schools of thought. On the one hand, a young generation of architects was to develop, rather cautiously, the line of Berlage's early work; A.J. Kropholler, for example, in his traditional brick architecture continued to refer to historical examples with a functional use of traditional materials. The proponents of this simple traditional use of materials were to come together later in the Delft School, around the professor M.J. Grandpré Molière. Their influence on later architecture was extremely large and lasted right into the 1960s, to then rapidly dwindle.

Opposed to these traditionalists were the younger architects who thought that Berlage did not go far enough, and who in the Nieuwe Bouwen aimed at a more functional architecture. They encountered a similar tendency towards further innovation among young colleagues abroad. They organised internationally in the Congrès Internationaux d'Architecture Moderne, the CIAM, whose founding meeting in 1928 in La Sarraz in Switzerland, was incidentally attended by Berlage.

Between these two extremes were the architects of the Amsterdam School, who thought Berlage's work too dogmatic, and too 'smooth'. They used brick in contrasting colours in a virtuoso form for apparently moulded building volumes. Modern building techniques were only used in a concealed fashion for large spans and complicated steel supports which were kept out of sight.

With the architects of De Stijl also, the construction was often subservient to the desired design. The Rietveld-Schröderhuis in Utrecht from 1924 showed that clearly. Gerrit Th. Rietveld (1888–1964) made the design together with his client Mrs Truus Schröder-Schräder (1889–1985). The spatial quality was concentrated on the transitions from interior to exterior. The construction of the house and studio however, was for the most part traditional: above-ground masonry with wooden floor constructions, even thought the plastered outer walls and some steel rails around the balconies suggested a more innovative use of materials.

The Nieuwe Bouwen

Ultimately, it was chiefly the architects of the Nieuwe Bouwen who were to inspire new developments, also internationally, which would greatly influence architecture in the second half of the twentieth century.

One of the most gifted architects of the Nieuwe Bouwen in

Beurs, Amsterdam, 1885. H.P. Berlage and Th. Sanders
Competition design in the second round

Beurs, Amsterdam, 1903. H.P. Berlage
Perspective of built design

Head offices De Nederlanden van 1845,
The Hague, 1927. H.P. Berlage
Facade after the 1954 extension

Beurs
Interior with clean masonry and visible steel trusses

Rietveld-Schröderhuis, Utrecht, 1924. G.Th. Rietveld in collaboration with Mrs T. Schröder-Schräder

Rietveld-Schröderhuis
Interior with corner window in which interior and exterior melt into each other

the Netherlands was Jan Duiker (1890–1935). During his short career he built a number of highpoints of the Nieuwe Bouwen. Between 1920 and 1925 he designed the Zonnestraal sanatorium in Hilversum. It was opened in 1928. The slender detailed concrete skeleton filled in with transparent steel windows and low parapets was to become a textbook example of the Nieuwe Bouwen, in which functions can clearly be read in the exterior. The transparent character was related to an optimal use of daylight in a hygienic environment where TB patients came to be cured. The definitive design consisted of the main building and four separate pavilions, two of which were built.

From the same period date the Nirwana block of flats in The Hague (1927) and the Openlucht school on the Cliostraat in Amsterdam (1928). These buildings too are remarkable for the clear use of the visible concrete construction filled in with glass walls, even if the Nirwana block does not quite achieve the transparent character of Zonnestraal. Another example of the Nieuwe Bouwen is the Van Nelle factory in Rotterdam by J.A. Brinkman (1902–1949) and L.C. van der Vlugt (1894–1936). Here the construction formed the basis for the greatest possible height in the working areas, to which end floors supported by mushroom columns were used. Around the concrete skeleton a curtain wall of light steel frames has been hung. Alongside the strictly functional transportation shafts of steel and glass there are also spatial and architectural accents to be found. Examples of these are mainly to be found in the office building with its set back entrance and a flat facade in which the main stairway is built projecting outward at some points. Form and function were linked inextricably but did not prevent a startling spatial impact.

The followers of the Nieuwe Bouwen had many international contacts, particularly with Germany in the context of the CIAM and the Bauhaus. One of the youngest participants in the first CIAM congress was Cornelis van Eesteren (1897–1988). Between 1930 and 1947 he played an important role in CIAM as chairman. In Amsterdam, Van Eesteren worked in the department of urban development where he could put the CIAM principles of urban design into practice. He was one of the leading designers of the General Expansion Plan (AUP) for Amsterdam, which was exhibited, in its design phase, during the fourth CIAM congress 'The functional city' on the ship the Patris and in Athens in 1933. The separation of housing, work, leisure and traffic were important principles in this modern expansion plan.

CIAM, Team X and Forum

Shortly after the Second World War, serious objections arose within the ranks of the CIAM to the Charter of Athens, which advocated a strict separation of functions in urban design and placed a one-sided emphasis on big, tall housing blocks in greenery with a high housing density. Although criticism had already been heard during the CIAM congresses in Hoddesdon (1951) and Aix-en-Provence (1953), it was the group of

CIAM members who prepared the tenth congress in Dubrovnik (1959) in particular, the so-called Team X, who lodged serious objections to the Athens Charter. They no longer saw urban design as a result of functions, but as a material form of relations[1].

Apart from Jaap Bakema and Aldo van Eyck, Team X consisted of Georges Candilis, Shadrach Woods, Rolf Gutmann, William Howell, Alison and Peter Smithson and John Völcker[2]. After the tenth CIAM congress in Dubrovnik, where the organization was officially disbanded, Team X convened the very last CIAM congress in Otterlo. Oscar Newman reported about the work of the architects present in Otterlo that some of them were 'aggressively' looking for a language which would communicate something of human behaviour in a more direct manner[3]. They were searching for a new architecture in which it was attempted to develop individual and social qualities.

The same critique was to be found among the younger generation of Dutch architects. They were confronted by the postwar housing shortage and the lack of building materials which resulted in monotonous new neighbourhoods with blocks of flats lower than four stories, to avoid having lifts. In a period when building was still carried out almost completely traditionally, the emphasis was on quantity.

The prewar studies in CIAM were mainly concerned with cheap housing for families with minimum incomes, so it could be worked out how expensive building land could continue to meet the basic requirements of healthy housing with the highest possible building density. After 1945, these minimum requirements quickly became the norm for social housing for a much larger section of the population than those who had to exist on the minimum income. The simple typologies with open blocks from the CIAM studies turned out to be ideal for the efficient realization of new expansion plans. Residential neighbourhoods in The Hague like Moerwijk and Morgenstond, after the urban design by Dudok, but also filling in of the western garden cities in Amsterdam's General Expansion Plan, were developed with simple typologies with open blocks. In this fashion, one after the other, new expansion plans were realised in order to eliminate the housing shortage as quickly as possible.

The critique of these rigid CIAM plans gained an unexpected platform at the end of the 1950s, in 'Forum, monthly journal for architecure and related arts'. The journal had been founded in 1946 by the association Architectura et Amicitia and the Association of Dutch Architects. Until the middle of 1959 its content consisted mainly of the selective documentation of architecture. Forum had also taken over the task from 'De 8 en Opbouw', as mouthpiece for the CIAM. For example, the Forum number for June/July 1952 had been completely devoted to the work of Dutch CIAM architects. Even then, some discontent could be heard with the social developments and their translation into the built environment. In this CIAM number Bakema wrote, inspired by the Hoddesdon congress: 'We feel

Openlucht school, Amsterdam, 1928. J. Duiker
The balconies form transitions between outside and
the schoolyard

Zonnestraal Sanatorium, Hilversum, 1928. J. Duiker and B. Bijvoet
Main building with the concrete skeleton as visible element of the architecture

Zonnestraal Sanatorium
Plan of complete design

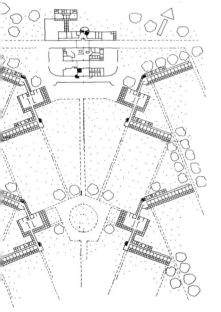

Nirwanaflat, The Hague, 1927. J. Duiker and J.G. Wiebenga

**Van Nelle factory, Rotterdam, 1929.
J.A. Brinkman and L.C. van der Vlugt**
The glass curtain wall is interrupted for
extensions with stairway landings

a lack of 'core' in society, and we know, that without this we can never be really free and happy'[4].

In the September number of 1959 the board of A et A noted that in the postwar years there had been feverish activity, with buildings being built for all kinds of purposes, especially many houses. But if one looked not only at statistics and production, then the question arose of whether the result was really the best response to the great housing shortage. The board of A et A spoke of a feeling of uneasiness which could not be repressed, which seemed to demand a critical reflection upon architects' own activities. That resulted in a new editorial board which started work in September 1959. This consisted of Dick Apon (1926), Aldo van Eyck (1918), Jaap Bakema (1914–1981), Gert Boon (1921), Joop Hardy (1918–1983), Herman Hertzberger (1932) and Jurriaan Schrofer for the typographic design.

The appearance of the first number under this editorial board coincided with the Team X congres in Otterlo.

Another idea

The new editors of Forum, who quickly came to be known as the Forum group, announced in the first number, under the slogan: 'The story of another idea', its dissatisfaction, particularly with the housing being built. Printed in bold, heavy type Aldo van Eyck advanced the proposition:

> *Seldom were the possibilities greater*
> *Seldom has a profession failed so badly*

Van Eyck argued that the Netherlands was threatened with becoming uninhabitable in the spatial sense. He sharply attacked his colleagues and accused architects and town planners of bearing a large share of the responsibility for making this little country uninhabitable. Van Eyck also settled accounts with the Athens Charter, which in his opinion had focused in too one-sided a manner on rudimentary principles in order to achieve a provisional partial organization. Bitterly, Van Eyck remarked: 'It was not "la Ville Radieuse" which convinced the planning official, but CIAM's "die funktionelle Stadt"...after low-rise and stacked dwellings, refuge was sought in high-rise. But there too, Le Corbusier's 1935 study "La Ville Radieuse" was not the model, because this trailblazer was "too individualistic for CIAM".'

As examples of another idea, urban designs for the Rotterdam suburbs of Pendrecht and Alexander polder were included, in which a construction became visible in smaller housing units which collectively formed a larger urban expansion. The housing units themselves were built up of neighbourhoods with villas, rows of single-family dwellings, flats, gallery flats, maisonettes and high-rise in order to achieve the best possible mixture of social groups.

In this number of Forum, new concepts and words were introduced into architecture and urban design. 'We are confronted by the task of creating inhabitable cities in a country which is already almost uninhabitable. True interiors of the community, so that everybody knows who and where he is, so that the sheltered spirit can heat the houses, streets and squares,' is how Van Eyck put it. In Hoddesdon, Bakema had already spoken of core, and defined it as follows: 'there are moments in our life when the distance between people and things is removed; at that moment we discover the miracle of relations between people and things. That is the moment of core, the moment in which we are aware of a fuller life by perceiving connections whose existence we had not been yet aware of.'[5]

Thus, the impressive first number of Forum under the new editors presented an image, not yet entirely sharply focussed, of the goals, as practical examples in architecture were not yet available. But the critique of the postwar housing environment was ready and clearly formulated.

Interior – exterior dialogue

'Threshold and encounter: the shape of the transition', was the title of the next number of Forum.[6] It states an essential fundamental idea of the Forum editors. The threshold, but also the window, are transitional areas between interior and exterior, if they are consciously designed as spatial transitions. Joop Hardy spoke of the 'kingdom of the transition.'

By stacking match boxes Hertzberger showed how rows of houses could be given a greater wealth of spatial transitions by shifting them around with regard to each other. By placing them at an angle, terraces and balconies suddenly acquire shelter from the neighbouring dwellings, but also a spatial border from the interior. Another example showed examples of terrace dwellings with bigger exterior spaces than the minimal balconies which were then the norm.

With an inimitably colourful choice of words Aldo van Eyck emphasised that it was more than merely a question of the transitions between interior and exterior. He wrote: 'make every door a greeting and every window a face. Do this now, because the proper kingdom of the spirit is the kingdom of the in-between, wealth of architecture. Make every window and every door a spot, a cluster of spots of every house and every city, and as well as this, make every house a little city and every city a big house. Build the counterform of the spirit for each and everyone, because they no longer do it themselves.'

Another housing

The trend-setting Forum editorial board was responsible for twenty three issues of the journal[7]. More than once, attention here was focussed on 'another housing'[8], as reaction to the bleak postwar functionalism in new urban expansions. As well as alternatives to straight blocks of single-family dwellings and small groups of dwellings with a mixture of various forms of housing, existing and new experiments were also published and examined in the light of the Forum idea.

As opposed to dwellings on narrow galleries with the minimum of lifts and simple railings as parapets, the housing of Michiel

Qu'il nous est difficile

Poser la question de l'Habitat moderne c'est poser le problème de l'art de vivre aujourd'hui.
Cet art existe-t-il?
[Le Corbusier, Aix, Ciam 9 — 1953]

Dit nummer is zowel een afsluiting als een begin. Aan het begin van dit begin behoren twee constateringen.
De eerste – dat Nederland er ruimtelijke om onbewoonbaar wordt – is een realiteit die zee tot het bewustzijn doordringt als de ademhaling komer wordt.
De tweede – dat architect en stedebouwer, wier bestaan en bestaansrecht op het heeft, respectievelijk gebruik van verbeelding en beeldend vermogen behoort te berusten, tot het onbewoonbaar maken van dit kleine land een zeer groot aandeel hebben – is een paradox die eindelijk aan het gewoten begint te knagen.

Zelden waren de mogelijkheden ruimer
Zelden heeft een vak zo gefaald

Tussen het leven dat door de kunst en de wetenschap bepaald wordt en het leven dat door regeringswetten en voorschriften wordt geregeld, staat een muur. Deze scheiding veroorzaakt groot verlies aan idealen en van menselijke activiteit.
Men moet de verbeeldingskracht als een niet te verwaarlozen element in de organisatie van de samenleving, weer in ear herstellen.
[Bakema, Dubrovnic, Ciam 10 — 1956]

Men blijve zich afvragen hoe het mogelijk is dat de mens niet meer in staat is datgene te maken wat hij krachtens zijn wezen voor alles behoort te kunnen maken, wisselende omstandigheden ten spijt: een eigen milieu waarin hij zichzelf herkennen kan, zijn voortbestaan kan waarborgen – zonder zijn identiteit te verloochenen.

feeling that you are somebody living somewhere

[Peter Smithson]

We are living as you know, in an age which is essentially technological, not really a scientific age. You've got to dig extraordinarily deep to find any philosophy ot aN dominating technological development.
[Dr. G. Scott Williamson, Hoddesdon, Ciam 8 — 1951]

Wij willen met dit nummer on de nummers die erop zullen volgen een beroep doen op uw gevoel, op uw verantwoordelijkheidsgevoel dus. De scheiding waarvan Bakema spreekt, is in, maar architecten en stedebouwers trekken naar het schijnt, tussen henzelf en hasgeen zij krachtens hun specifieke taak te doen hebben, een andere scheiding opgevonzoen. Zij hebben tussen hun kunstenaarschap en hzrzelf onvrijde, hun kunstenaarschap en de gemeenschap onderijde een wereld van onbewerkelijkheid doen ontstaan waarin tot onheil van henzelf en de gemeenschap hun kunstenaarschap is weggezonken.

Aan de rand van de aandacht staat steeds de kunstenaar, wezenlijk bondgenoot van het kind. Zijn functie is nog le docoratief. [Hij wordt misbruikt en misbruikt zichzelf.] Zijn vak is het tot stand brengen van verbeelde orde, zijn plaats is in het midden.
[Aldo van Eyck, Dubrovnic, Ciam 10 — 1956]

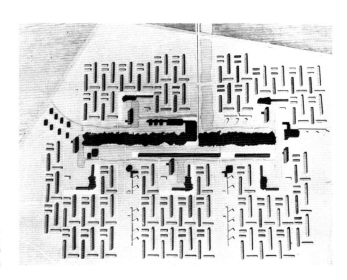

Urban design Rotterdam-Pendrecht, 1949, Opbouw
CIAM entry for the congress in Bergamo, 1949, and published in Forum, September 1959, as an example of repetition of small housing units

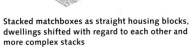

Stacked matchboxes as straight housing blocks, dwellings shifted with regard to each other and more complex stacks

Brinkman in Rotterdam-Spangen from 1921 was put forward, where the galleries had expanded into elevated streets where the baker and dairyman brought their carts up with them in the lift[9]. Together with Hans Hollein, Bakema discovered the housing architecture of Rudolph Schindler and in Forum, reported enthusiastically on the multiplicity of transitional areas between interior and exterior. He also pointed out how Schindler had found an opportunity to make the American building system of 'wooden skeleton construction' as structuring construction visible on the exterior[10].

Designs by Team X members for housing were published as a response to the quest for 'another housing', such as the 'terraced housing units' of Alison and Peter Smithson[11], a city on poles by Ralph Erskine[12] and a preliminary study by Moshe Safdie for his later experiment 'Habitat '67', which with prefabricated three-dimensional elements and new entrances would be built on the occasion of the World Fair in Montreal.[13] With some of his own designs, Bakema showed how he wanted to put the philosophy of 'another housing' into practice. The Kennemerland plan was an example of urban design on a regional scale[14]. Bakema also published an extendable dwelling for the neighbourhood of 't Hool in Eindhoven. This dwelling links up with the Dutch tradition of rows of single-family dwellings but can easily be extended with the growth of the family living in it. 'Determining the structure for the growing house are the transverse walls with pipes for water, sewage, electricity. Between these walls and a minimum building line, core spaces are defined for the beginning family, with living, cooking, sleeping, storage. These cores are all equal and laid out linearly, they are mass produced by a communal product economy. For expansion of this core wall a number of possibilities have been designed, in consultation with the housing corporation and municipal departments. The extensions can be made with prefabricated elements, in three-dimensional modules, and they are bordered by the maximum building line'[15], according to the commentary.

Despite all the interest in these more or less experimental housing forms, the practice of housing architecture, according to Aldo van Eyck, continued to degenerate into uninhabitable new buildings. He observed: 'Today it is a question of finding large significant structures, which are recognizable to all city-dwellers, and continue to be so, and in which every city-dweller can recognise himself through what he meaningfully adds, or changes, from place to place and from day to day, freely and in accordance with his own real needs.'[16] This notion linked up directly to a quotation which was published a number of times in Forum, from Wim van Bodegraven who in 1952 at a preparatory meeting for CIAM in Sigtuna noted: 'We support the need to create a structure or forms, which can further develop with time; which remain a whole of forms in both their beginning and their further growth and maintain the coherence of the parts. The lack of this has to lead to self-destruction.'[17]

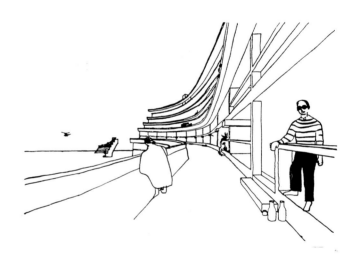

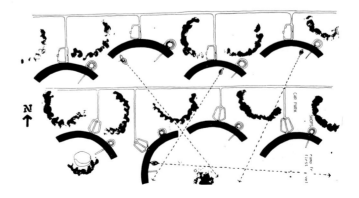

Terraced housing units. Alison and Peter Smithson
A study plan exhibited during the CIAM congress in Otterlo

Design of 'growing dwellings', around 1962. Van den Broek and Bakema

Design of 'growing dwellings', around 1962. Van den Broek and Bakema
The dwellings with supporting walls which continue outside made extensions on the ground floor easy.
A roof storey could also be added

'Habitat', Montreal, 1967. Moshe Safdie
Preliminary studies of this residential neighbourhood built up
from stacked spatial elements were published in Forum

Orphanage in Amsterdam

Aldo van Eyck's Burgerweeshuis, completed in 1960, can be regarded as a built counterform of the ideas of the Forum editors, the Forum idea. But it also formed a starting point of Dutch structuralism, as that would be developed in various directions, especially by students associated with the Amsterdam School of Architecture. Soon after completion the Burgerweeshuis received international recognition and was positively received.

In his commentary 'The gentle etching of reciprocity'[18], Van Eyck explained that he been looking for an open community, from which the children could visit schools, courses and associations in the city, but to which they could also bring friends. For the changing residents, spaces were designed for specific age groups.

The building consists of a number of self-contained housing units around an inner street, which together form a whole. In this fashion Van Eyck wanted to reconcile a centralist lay-out with a dispersed decentralization. In its main design, the complex was given a fanciful form in order to allow as much morning and afternoon sun in as possible. Sheltering outside spaces with projecting roofs ensure transitions between interior and exterior which are both turned outward and self-contained. These transitions are developed in various ways but nevertheless form a unity through the use of the same materials. Within a single style, Aldo van Eyck achieved for the residents a changing interplay of views outward, and vistas in and around the patios inside the building.

The Burgerweeshuis inspires a reconsideration of apparent opposites, such as many – single, unity – diversity, element – whole, big – small, many – few, inside – outside, closed – open, movement – rest, constancy – change, individual – community, and so on. Van Eyck calls these differences 'dual phenomena', which he tries to reconcile with each other. The numerous small domes and some larger ones show how multiplicity is reconciled with unity and unity with diversity by repetition of the basic form.

Van Eyck has written about this as follows: 'The intention was to create a spot, a bunch of spots through recognition of the healing power of reciprocity, where the split dual phenomena are given a great opportunity to restore themselves… In the present city everything is too big and too small, too distant and too nearby, too much and too little, too much and too little the same, too much and too little different. Therefore everything was aimed at an attempt to build this orphanage like a small city, on the basis of the recognition that the city should be like a big house. Here, a multiplicity of elements were permitted, so to speak, to form a loose, complex pattern. They were then all subjected to a single structural and constructional principle in order to make the pattern recognizable and homogeneous, and also joined together by a general human motif with an individual/ community significance: the inner street with adjoining exterior areas. While all the spaces independent of their function and span conform to the possibilities of a single architectural style, each is given specific meaning by its position, purpose, order, treatment of detail, by their relation to each other, the whole and the content of the situation. As far as consciously giving a form to the transitional area is concerned, this goes together as a matter of course with all the ideas mentioned here; the weave of ideas out of which this orphanage was created. The goal was to set a home for children in the context of architecture.'[19]

Structure

The Burgerweeshuis is built up according to a clearly recognizable construction which has remained visible throughout the entire building. On the ground floor there are round concrete columns in a fixed pattern, with over them prefabricated joists as architraves. These architraves are provided with a spacious horizontal opening which is glazed in the outer walls and often left open on the interior. They rest on the columns, or where columns have been left out, on loadbearing brickwork.

Between the columns are big glass walls or glass bricks. The eaves are on the architraves with behind them the characteristic prefabricated concrete domes, with between them concrete joists poured on the spot as linking constructions on the architraves.

The brickwork is in doubly thick red brick, in which the stacking of the bricks can more easily be distinguished through the greater thickness than is the case with the usual narrower brick, the so-called 'Waal' brick.

The storey above the entrance to the forecourt contains accommodation for the staff. For groups of children older than ten years, the sleeping accommodation is also situated on the upper level. They are roof constructions of a single storey, built completely in concrete.

Gerrit Rietveld placed Van Eyck's Burgerweeshuis accurately in the Dutch architectural tradition when he wrote to him: 'I think the floor plan of your building on the Amstelveenseweg is masterly. It is perceived both inside and outside. I remember a discussion with Berlage during the setting up of the congress in La Sarraz when he said: you are destroying what I am building up (he did not participate with us). I feel like saying to you: you are building up what I destroyed, because your heavy brick and the concrete lintels remind me so much of Berlage. I hope that your enthusiasm will prevent so-called functionalism becoming bourgeois.'[20]

As well as Berlage's 'honest' use of materials, the Burgerweeshuis is also clearly reminiscent of the visible skeleton of Duiker's Zonnestraal and the Openlucht school. The rectangular wall surfaces of brick seem to refer to the most striking designs of De Stijl. The overall construction of the Burgerweeshuis reminded Jürgen Joedicke of Louis Kahn's fundamental principle, that an architectural space must show how it has been made.[21] The domes on the roof are also expressive of Van Eyck's intense interest in African communities, such as the Dogon in the Sahara,

Burgerweeshuis, Amsterdam, 1960. Aldo van Eyck
Load-bearing masonry alternates with a concrete skeleton, filled in with glass bricks and glass walls

Burgerweeshuis
Inner street with alternating access of daylight and view

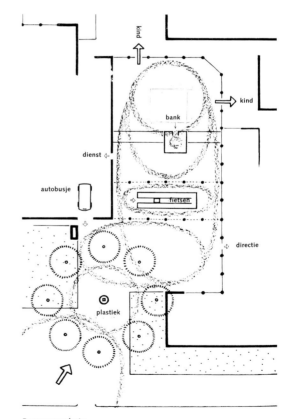

Burgerweeshuis
Spatial transitions between transitions which flow into each other, between city and front door

Burgerweeshuis
Forms of the 'architecure style', according to Francis Strauven

which he visited together with Herman Haan, many photos of which he published in Forum to illustrate his articles.

The Burgerweeshuis, therefore, was in the first instance a built manifesto of the Forum idea. At the same time, the clearly visible skeleton inspired a profound reconsideration among some members of the young generation of architects in the Netherlands. The way in which Van Eyck used the skeleton as a structuring construction in his architecture, put these architects on a new trail, which would lead to a wide range of development, with completely individual interpretations.

Space-structuring construction

Piet Blom and Joop van Stigt were finalists for the Prix de Rome in 1962. Although Blom won the prize, it is chiefly the design by Joop van Stigt which was of importance for the rising structuralism, through its use of a space-structuring construction. For the design of 'a village for children', he chose a structural combination of a 'basic form' from which the floor plans were built up, with a comparatively complicated construction plan of columns, joists, balustrades and walls. In early study sketches Van Stigt had already discovered that the configuration of partially overlapping rectangles offered possibilities, thorough mutual linkage, for flexible usage in which functions were simply interchangeable. The desire for flexibility was characteristic of the 1960s, although in the Burgerweeshuis specific spaces for children of different ages had been specially asked for. Van Stigt was very familiar with the orphanage as he had been involved in its construction as site engineer. His children's village was much bigger and led to a more complex construction in which big spaces, including a hall for six hundred people, were enclosed by building volumes which were also built up from the basic form of a double square or a plural of this. In this way a conglomeration of interior and exterior spaces around streets, courtyards and squares which dropped in height at their edges as a transition to the surrounding landscape, was created. In explanation, Joop van Stigt wrote: 'With elements of a small order the more detailed specific function of housing, working, sleeping is defined, differentiated by use and coinciding with the structure.'[22]

This construction from smaller elements in combination with a space-structuring and architecture-defining construction would later be further developed in a structuralist sense by Herman Hertzberger in particular, in various large briefs.

The winning design by Piet Blom also consisted of a configurational structured design with numerous squares surrounded by building, but the construction was traditional, in brickwork. Apon wrote in Forum about both designs: 'The real importance of the achievement of Blom and Van Stigt is that they show us in an inspiring fashion the changing process, in which the defining of simple forms gives way to that of the formal and spatial structure.'[23] Blom used the Forum idea, Van Stigt developed it further into a constructive spatial structure.

In 1962, the town planning supervisors of the University of Twente (then still the Polytechnic) W. van Tijen and S.J. van Embden, commissioned both Prix de Rome participants for the Campus Drienerlo. In order to keep the memory of the country estate alive, it was decided to preserve a former farmhouse and convert it into a temporary student restaurant. Blom replaced the simple roof with a roofscape of sloping roofs with ceramic tiles that together with the new wooden construction formed a structuring element in the mostly new building. With the help of a series of voids a large number of 'spots' were created, which at various points displayed a direct spatial relation with the exterior by means of high windows. Terraces and garden fences formed a further transition of the building to the green surroundings.

Van Stigt was given the brief for a staff canteen. He used a configuration of four cruciform basic structures. In constructive terms, these were translated into a laminated wooden construction. As the windows are included directly in the wooden construction, a clearly readable construction was created in the very transparent building. Here, at a very early stage, Joop van Stigt had already achieved in an expert fashion a prototype of a structuring construction.

Town halls as houses in the city

Herman Hertzberger seized the opportunity to further define the Forum idea and the structuralism which arose from it in a number of large designs for two town halls and the head offices of an insurance company. In 1961 he was invited to participate in a multiple commission for a town hall in Valkenswaard, in which Dick Apon was another participant.[24] In his unrealized design Hertzberger was aiming at an anti-monumental town hall 'where public and officials come to visit each other.'[25] On the basis of a grid with square 'towers' and voids between them a more developed configuration of squares cut open at the corners around even bigger voids, mutually connected by bridges, was created. The design could be built in phases and could be extended with new towers or an extra floor at some points. The office landscape which was in fashion in the 1960s as a replacement for the inflexible office with small workrooms, was given a new dimension in Hertzberger's design by forming relations between the various floors. The articulation of the floor plan made it difficult, if not impossible, to pile up offices if the number of officials were to grow. In this design, working in a single unarticulated office landscape was exchanged for an 'individual work station' within the greater whole.

By freely manipulating the grid Hertzberger was also able to include the marriage and council halls within the main layout of the chosen configuration. The strong articulation of the building volume was also an elegant gesture towards the existing small-scale buildings in the centre of Valkenswaard.

For the international competition for the Amsterdam town hall in 1967, Hertzberger further developed the concept from Valkenswaard. In the configuration he returned to square towers with a cruciform void at the corners. A new element was the

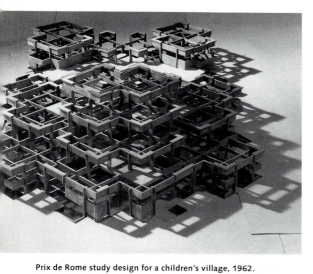

**Prix de Rome study design for a children's village, 1962.
Joop van Stigt**
Maquette of a loadbearing construction

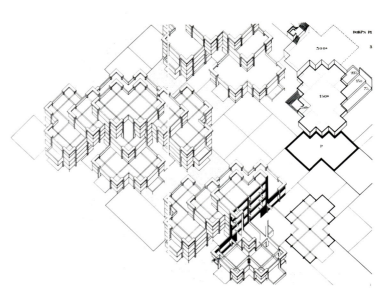

Prix de Rome 1962. Joop van Stigt

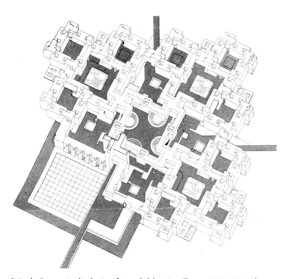

Prix de Rome study design for a children's village, 1962. Piet Blom
An urban fabric around inner courts in which the bearing construction
is strikingly present

Former student restaurant, University of Twente, Enschede, 1964. Piet Blom
New roofs form a structuring element in the design of the converted farmhouse

Former staff canteen University of Twente, Enschede, 1964. Joop van Stigt
Because of the all-round glazing the structure of the building remains recognizable

rotation of the grid towards the diagonal of the buildings site, so that pedestrian routes through the building could be included as a useful addition to the urban fabric. Through this positioning serrated facades were created which emphatically linked up with the modal lot widths of the Amsterdam canal houses around the design.

For the council hall and the auditorium bigger building volumes were needed. Hertzberger accommodated these in round building volumes which, because of their central position within the structure, do not interfere with the scale adjustment towards the exterior.

Although Hertzberger's design was particularly highly regarded in professional circles,[26] the jury rejected the design in the first round. This also happened to two other structuralist designs by Gert Boon and Jan Verhoeven. The design by Boon, who like Hertzberger was an editor of Forum, showed, in the larger scale configuration chosen, a strong reciprocity between the open space of the city and the town hall.

Of the seven designers who were allowed to further develop their entries for the Amsterdam town hall in a second round, Leo Heijdenrijk was the only Dutch architect. In order to meet criticism of his design from the first round, Heijdenrijk made extensive changes to his plan. The square towers, almost fifteen metres high, of his second design showed a remarkable similarity to Hertzberger's town hall design for Valkenswaard. However, the construction of Heijdenrijk's design was based on a completely different principle, with in the centre of each tower four columns which supported a lattice of beams which was raised in height towards the edges of the towers. Although Heijdenrijk's towers were parallel to the edges of the site, the bank of the Amstel and the Zwanenburgwal were diagonally cut off under the building and broadened in order to interweave the water with the buildings.

The built manifesto

With the brief for the head offices of the insurance company Centraal Beheer, Herman Hertzberger was given the opportunity to test in practice the philosophy behind the town hall designs for Valkenswaard and Amsterdam. Once again the towers are in the corners of the plan, with diagonal main traffic routes, which as public space link up with the station which was planned at the passageway between the office building beside it, by Wim Davidse (which also has a floor plan of diagonal squares with structuralist features).

What is noticeable in the design for Centraal Beheer is the free way in which the pattern has been treated. The columns of the office floors are supported in the garage under the building, four at a time, by a single, heavy, mushroom-shaped construction column, with the direction of the construction being rotated fifty degrees. On the columns along the edges of the square floor surfaces of the towers are beams which bear a part of two floor surfaces (that is, towers) with on them the floor surfaces which again cover a single tower. In this way the structural

grids shift constantly as a complication of the chosen form. The same reciprocity is encountered in the installations and in use. Each tower floor has four work areas in the corners which are reached by aisles over the bridges; the wiring follows the access routes via the bridges and are refined into local infills for ceiling heating and lighting. In this way, in the terminology of Aldo van Eyck, an ordered chaos is created, although Hertzberger sometimes gives the impression of looking for a greater clarity, such as Duiker and Bijvoet achieved in Zonnestraal and the Openlucht school[27].

Characteristics of structuralism

Structuralism in the Netherlands developed in the course of the years and is still adapting to new developments in society as they influence building. For example, flexibility hardly played a role in Aldo van Eyck's Burgerweeshuis, because the client asked for spaces designed specifically for different age groups. A few years later Joop van Stigt recognized the growing demand for flexibility in his design for the Prix de Rome, a principle which was further developed by Herman Hertzberger in his town hall designs and the Centraal Beheer Building. In these extremely divergent designs a space-structuring construction was applied which was left visible both inside and outside. This attention to *growth and cohesion* was to become an important characteristic of the emerging structuralism. The Forum idea, as that was propagated by the editorial board between 1959 and 1963, laid the emphasis mainly on the attunement of the housing and working environment to specific human needs. The *building from the encounter* became a leading purpose designers.

In looking for a further enrichment of the achievement with regard to light and air dating from the CIAM period, a housing environment was aimed at in which both the possibilities for personal privacy and the encounter by the inhabitant himself could be given shape. In this, new building methods made a varied construction possible which led to all kinds of geometric configurations and *mutual attachment* became possible.

As a reaction to CIAM the rigid monofunctional aspect of residential districts was transformed into a mixture of functions. As examples, the structuralist pointed to inner cities in which through years and sometimes centuries of use colour changes have become visible, and where users took advantage of the chances to give a more individual shape to their built environment. In this quest for a richly assorted life the structuralists sought *multiple land use and urban insertions*.

Because the characteristics of structuralism were not always equally clearly present in the various designs, in the past there were quite a few misunderstandings about whether a building could or could not be attributed to structuralism. Herman Hertzberger remarked about this: 'Everything which is put together, no matter how ramshackle, is quickly given the name of structure... Everything in architecture, good or bad, where the construction is visually to the fore, and which involves repeti-

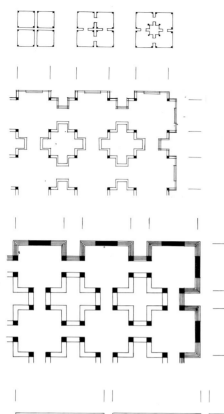

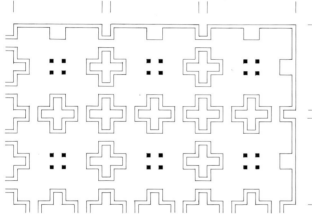

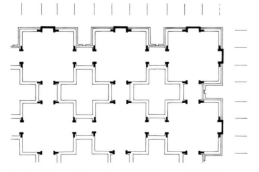

Configurations of three town hall designs and Centraal Beheer on the same scale. From the top down: Valkenswaard town hall, 1966, Herman Hertzberger; Amsterdam town hall, 1968, Herman Hertzberger; Amsterdam town hall, second round, 1968, Leo Heijdenrijk; Centraal Beheer, Apeldoorn, 1972, Herman Hertzberger

Head offices Centraal Beheer, Apeldoorn, 1972. Herman Hertzberger

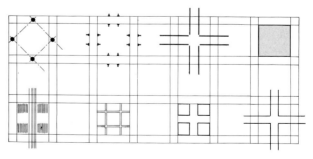

Head offices Centraal Beheer
Different-sized grids on the basis of which the building was designed; above, from left to right: columns of lower storey with parking, columns of upper building, floor beams and the floor plate; below: wiring above the ceiling, ceiling, four work places and access to them

tion of concrete components, prefabricated or not, grids and skeletons, taut or lacking cohesion or both, is stored in the structuralism drawer.'[28]

Growth and cohesion: the visible construction

In structuralism, the construction is more than merely a support for the efficient building of a design, to be afterwards hidden from view. Revealing a skeleton shows the users of the building how the building has been made, as Duiker and Bijvoet showed the skeleton in Zonnestraal and Berlage did in the office building for De Nederlanden van 1845. With bigger buildings a visible construction gives the user more insight into the real dimensions and a recognisable rhythm is created which provides insight into the overall number of repetitions. If such a skeleton is kept out of the way behind brickwork, plasterwork or slabs, then only the large volume remains and there is a lack of reference for the real dimensions.

Growth and cohesion demand simple expandability and possibilities for interchangability. The loadbearing construction of structuralist buildings can therefore be expanded relatively simply. The desire for internal flexibility usually involves a division between loadbearing and space-dividing functions, between bearer and infill components. That often has implications for the facades, which must also be adaptable. Frank van Klingeren situated the multifunctional community centre 't Karregat in such a way that expansion could take place on all sides and the functions within the building were interchangeable. In the Hogeschool in Delft by Jan Tennekes the building sections are completely interchangeable. In the housing complex by Otto Steidle in Munich, which is closely related to Dutch structuralism, the skeleton was even continued further, so that inhabitants could simply acquire extra space by filling in a new piece of the open skeleton with floors, walls and facades. This idea was not new; in the first half of the 1930s Le Corbusier designed the project 'Fort l'Empereur' for Algiers. Continuous floors with a space between them two stories high, based on columns, offered possibilities of individual filling in of the dwellings according to the inhabitant's taste. The street was also included in this superstructure.

Structuralists are free in their treatment of a skeleton. The columns of Hertzberger's Muziekcentrum Vredenburg are sometimes completely inside the facades and a little further on completely outside. In doing so he wanted to exploit all the possibilities of construction which could enrich the overall image, even if he was of the opinion that the construction had to be completely sound. As opposed to this, Aldo van Eyck suggested that the search for a valid system can be seen as 'a search for permanence, while for this you have to pay the price of excluding a lot of possibilities.'[29] In the Muziekcentrum, a number of 'standard columns' bear the roof construction of the big concert hall with a considerable span whereby the amount of reinforcement in the columns is greater than the amount of concrete around them. In this way Herman Hertzberger used

this freedom of manipulating the construction as Le Corbusier had already demonstrated in 1915 with his Domino system for dwellings, in which walls could be both joined to columns or kept separate from them.

In the 1980s, the need for energy conservation led to the adjustment of the principle of keeping the construction visible in the outer walls. A massive concrete column forms a kind of cold conductor in the midst of masonry with isolation in the cavity and glass walls with thermally separated inner and outer frames around the double glass. This was a reason for placing the construction once again within the outer wall, as happened with the extension of Estec and the Ministry of Education and Science in Zoetermeer. In this situation an elevation design is often sought which gives an indication of the place where the columns stand behind the facade.

Built from the encounter

People are central to Dutch structuralism, with the emphasis on mutual encounter and patterns of relations of users and the built environment. On the micro level of the building or elements of it, many facilities have been built in which invite mutual contacts. The concept of 'inner street', which first made its appearance in the Burgerweeshuis was further developed by Herman Hertzberger in the old people's centre De Drie Hoven. Here he designed a covered courtyard where low walls dividing the space also invite you to sit down for a chat or to look at the activities of others. In this way, for many people the house becomes a piece of the city with the specific spots and spatial continuity advocated by Van Eyck. Notable too in De Drie Hoven were the half-doors for the housing units: inhabitants can cut themselves off definitively by keeping the door completely closed, but they can also open the upper door a little for some visual contact with the corridor or completely open in order to have a conversation over the lower door with a neighbour.

In structuralism much importance is attached to the individual recognizability of the individual's living or working space. This is relevant to both the block of flats and the single-family-dwelling. It is precisely in the transitional area from dwelling to exterior that an individual contribution seems to be possible. For example, in various housing projects Herman Hertzberger designed balconies which make it possible to withdraw into a sheltered corner or look for contact with the neighbors thorough a conversation over the parapet. The interior of Centraal Beheer was consciously not finished in order to challenge users to make the space of their own work area their own with plants, photos or posters brought from home.

On the town planning level too, 'habitability' is a constantly recurring catchword and there is a reaction to lack of scale. It is therefore often unjustly assumed that structuralists would rather not make big buildings. Hertzberger states: 'Things must only be big as a multiple of units which are small in themselves, for excess soon creates an effect of distance and by always

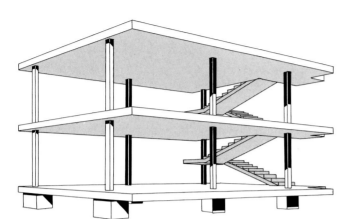

Domino houses, 1914–1915. Le Corbusier
The skeleton makes a free layout of the floor plan possible

Multi-functional community centre 't Karregat, Eindhoven, 1973. Frank van Klingeren
In the extendable skeleton the walls and functions of interiors are interchangeable

Project 'Fort l'Empereur' for Algiers, 1935. Le Corbusier
Inhabitants were invited to take possession of part of the structure

Muziekcentrum Vredenburg, Utrecht, 1979. Herman Hertzberger
The columns vary between being inside and outside the complex, but are always visible

De Drie Hoven, Amsterdam, 1974. Herman Hertzberger
Residents can individually determine their surroundings and degree of contact

making everything too big, too empty, and thus too distant and untouchable, architects are producing in the first place distance and inhospitality. Big as plural implies increasing complexity and therefore enrichment of interpretative possibilities through the great diversity of relationships in the ensemble of separate units from which the big whole is built up.'[30]

Mutual connections

The term configuration was much used within the Forum group. From the desire for housing forms more attuned to the inhabitants, connections were sought which would replace the ranks of square blocks of dwellings from CIAM studies, often typology and density studies which became the norm in postwar urban design. By shifting dwellings with regard to each other, terraces were created which had more privacy and were protected from the wind. The connection here is often based on constructive units or basic forms in the floor plan. In Joop van Stigt's Prix de Rome design, it emerged clearly in the repetition of two diagonally overlapping squares and their mutual stacking in relation to the loadbearing construction. The cruciforms in the structure of his staff canteen are another example of it. But in Hertzberger's designs for town halls and also Centraal Beheer, the structure consisted of a repetition of identical towers as constructive units, which because of the equilateral squares can be connected on two sides.

Multiple use

In Dutch structuralism it is often attempted to introduce an excess of details in order to stimulate multi-functional use. A somewhat bigger covered space at a junction of corridors can give rise to extra activities. Low walls inside or outside a building, or column bases, stairs or deep window-sills can through being slightly oversized contribute to multi-functional use as seating or offer space for children to play in. Illustrative of this is the protruding brickwork or overhang at a front door: while looking for the key you can put your shopping bag on this for a moment, the postman puts a package on it while the receipt is signed, children clamber up on it in order to press the bell and adults sit in the sun for a moment or put a flowerbox on it. Sometimes this desire for flexible use links up with the housing desires. In Hertzberger's diagoon dwellings only the stairs and sanitary facilities are fixed in the floor plan. Inhabitants themselves can decide whether they want to live or sleep at the front, the back, above or below. That was possible in a single open floor plan around the centre of the dwelling, where activities influence each other or in rooms which can be demarcated by building in dividing walls. Interchange of functions also remains possible during the process of use.

A much discussed example of multiple use was the multi-functional community centre 't Karregat by Frank van Klingeren, in which he wanted to 'de-lump' society. To this end various functions such as primary schools, shops, pubs and restaurants and library were housed under a single roof and these were partly

in an open relation to each other. In doing this Van Klingeren aimed to achieve a stimulating interweaving of school and library, of pubs and restaurants and waiting parents or participants in health care. In its impulse it formed a victory over the division of functions as championed by CIAM, and was incidentally greatly adjusted in later renovations.

Urban insertion and multiple land use

The insertion of contemporary buildings into existing urban neighbourhoods and inner cities was an often recurring theme in structuralism. It was Van Eyck above all who propagated a conscientious urban renewal in which he proposed repair of the original urban fabric with streets, alleys and building lines, often after substantial demolition. Central to this were contemporary architecture and scale adjustment, which Hertzberger and Heijdenrijk were also aiming at in their designs for the Amsterdam town hall. In the Vredenburg Muziekcentrum it was attempted to bring together on amicable terms the fine-grained old inner city and the large-scale Hoog Catharijne with strongly interwoven functions like shops, concert halls and pubs and restaurants around an arcade two stories high. When, during construction, fragments of the seventeenth century castle Vredenburg were found, adjustments were made for them both inside and outside the building and they were visually included as a memory of a piece of the city's history. Another example is the Kasbah in Hengelo, originally designed by Piet Blom to be built on a site in the inner city. The dwellings are raised above the ground level in order to be able to use this for parking, storage, a community centre, shops and greenery. Blom expected to be able to realise a strong mixture of housing, shopping and leisure with this 'urban roof' and so exploit the land twice over. Originally a second grid had been contemplated over the highways, with roads for pedestrians and perhaps the carts of the bakers and milkmen who still delivered to your home. The dwellings were linked in blocks to terraces and large urban inner spaces. In this design phase of 'the urban roof' Blom did not rule out the possibility of more intermediate floors with communal facilities and work opportunities.

In Rotterdam Blom built similar 'layered' buildings, bridging the Blaak. There is a broad highway on the ground level. To cross it, a bridge was built with at the edges spaces for small shops, boutiques and bars and restaurants. The actual pole dwellings, which are housed in tilted cubes, are reached by means of steps around small storage areas. Although the tilted dwelling forms form a configuration with each other the design cannot be called structuralist because of the lack of a space-structuring construction and the not very flexible layout of the dwellings; the multiple land use is only fragmentarily applied here.

Urban grids

The characteristics of structuralism which have already been described were developed in very different ways. For example, in the Centraal Beheer Herman Hertzberger was already using

Experimental housing De Kasbah, Hengelo, 1973. Piet Blom
Multiple ground use with dwellings above the access streets and parking

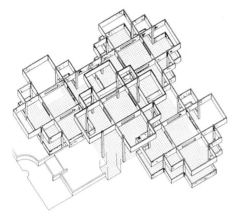

Staff canteen University of Twente, 1964. Joop van Stigt
Cruciform basic elements in the wooden constructions linked together

Multi-functional community centre 't Karregat, Eindhoven, 1973. Frank van Klingeren
School interior with open group spaces which are only separated by half-height cupboards

Building across the Blaak with pole dwellings, Rotterdam, 1984. Piet Blom
A bridge across a traffic route for pedestrians with shops and housing above them

a layered construction where the functions were expressed in construction and use within the chosen configuration in squares on a grid. On a city scale Piet Blom did the same with his 'urban roof', with street level, pedestrian traffic and dwellings. They formed grids, so to speak,which were laid on and across each other. The reasons for this multi-functional use of the land were mainly connected with the quickly expanding urban building which was at the cost of landscapes and open space, and which could be limited by multiple use of the land. The reaction to the separation of functions championed by CIAM also played a leading role. That could be seen, for example, from a 'Study for an urban grid' by the students Sake de Boer, Jos Mol, Iraj Parvin and Henk Reijenga from the Amsterdam School of Architecture, under the guidance of Herman Hertzberger.[31] In their commentary they objected to the splitting up of functions of planned roads, blocks, greenery and building regulations in municipal expansion plans in the Netherlands. This planning had to be replaced by a generative form of interplay of elements, extendability and in each phase a completed form. The organising grid which was sought would have to be open to individual interpretation for diverse functions and replace the traditional extension plan. The study plan was an attempt to introduce structuralism on an urban design level as a basis for the succeeding planning phase with building designs.

In 1968, the Tijdschrift voor Architectuur en Beeldende Kunst, which until 1967 had been called Katholiek Bouwblad, set an ideas competition for church-building.[32] The point of departure was the search for new forms of church building. For the Utrecht neighbourhood of Overvecht a church space for 600 worshippers was required. Leo Heijdenrijk got the first prize for an extremely rough design, 'Kresko'. On a two-sided grid of almost seven metres he had developed a structure with a load-bearing construction where all kinds of community facilities could be housed, including the church space, on a number of floors, around a pedestrian entrance raised above ground level. The rough design formed an interesting example of an urban grid, which in this case was 'knitted into' a postwar residential neighbourhood, but which could also serve as a structuralist bearer of communal facilities for new neighbourhoods. The design had a realistic engineering structure which was reminiscent of superstructures by artists like Yona Friedman and Constant Nieuwenhuys.

For Scheveningen, Heijdenrijk developed a somewhat less extreme design which was not built either. Above an underground car park to the south of the Kurhaus a number of floors of shops with bars and restaurants were envisaged, and dwellings above them. In the various grids above each other a configuration was created, from the parking facilities under the entrance zone upward, of rectangles which further developed into open squares with terrace dwellings. The daylight would penetrate deep into the parking space through voids. The design could be simply extended outside the actual planning area,

in which more extensive innovations were forecast at the time. It was Herman Hertzberger who put structuralism into practice on a city level with his Muziekcentrum Vredenburg as a link between the large-scale Hoog Catharijne and the finely-meshed fabric of the Utrecht inner city. The shopping consumers and train passengers are relegated to the raised shopping centre at the foot of the offices and a block of flats, for the sake of efficient traffic. Hertzberger succeeded in housing shops, bars and restaurants in two floors around the concert halls. The terraced structure and the visible construction with diverse infills ensured a successful connection with the scale of the inner city. A fascinating spatial transition was created between inner and outer spaces with between them the arcade as a covered shopping street two stories high. The 'bunch of spots' which Aldo van Eyck had argued for in Forum, can here be encountered on an urban scale. Opponents have claimed that structuralists have contributed little to the development of urban design; Muziekcentrum Vredenburg is an example of careful insertion of new building which links up with the finely-woven fabric of the inner city, where the traffic routes through existing buildings originally planned have been avoided.

Diversity in practice
With the building of Centraal Beheer and Vredenburg, Hertzberger formulated and put into practice the leading characteristics of structuralism in the Netherlands in the 1970s. As well as this, the work of other architects, often on a smaller scale, gave a rich assortment to the many-sided development of structuralism. A notable example is Aldo van Eyck's Hubertushuis in Amsterdam. The entire complex of existing building and the new building at the front and rear linking up with it shows the principle of the Forum idea. The new building at the front in particular, with a concrete skeleton which has been unusually freely interpreted in scale, and which turns into steel at some points, once again makes it clear how Van Eyck picks up all the potential of the skeleton without clinging to an over-logically implemented system of scale. In his detached house in Retie the free interpretation of the main construction can be seen, with surprising transitions between inner and outer in a continuous structure of wood.

In the library by Wim Davidse in Doetinchem the size of the building task limited repetition of the constructive grid. The 'building from the encounter' is very clearly to be seen in the spatial relations whereby everyone can see each other and there are sufficient places to have a quick chat. This spatial continuity of interior spaces is continued in the immediate surroundings with flower pots and low walls. The concrete construction seems to be influenced by the concrete architecture of the Swiss architect Walter Förderer, as the outer walls with the skeleton have been made with concrete poured on the spot.

With Onno Greiner too, the construction is a criterion for the structure of his designs, but this is hardly to be seen from the

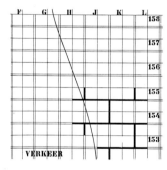

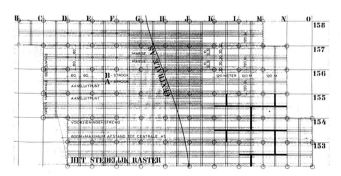

Study plan for an urban grid near Apeldoorn, 1968. Sake de Boer, Jos Mol, Iraj Parvin and Henk Reijenga
Grid for utilities with connections at the intersections of 120 X 120 metres, around the slightly curved central axis

Building in the A-strips and open ground level in the B-strips with a variable margin between them

Traffic grid of T-formed junctions as access

The complete urban grid

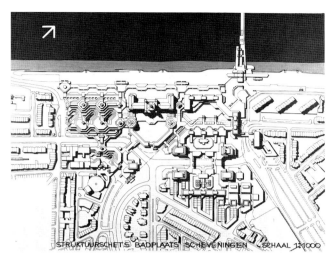

Structural plan of Scheveningen, 1974. Leo Heijdenrijk
Plan for block to the southwest of the Kurhaus with parking, shops and housing

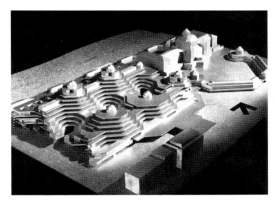

Structural plan Scheveningen
Maquette

Muziekcentrum Vredenburg, Utrecht, 1979. Herman Hertzberger
Arcade with shops and cafes/restaurants on ground floor and first floor

27

outside; only a strong articulation of the building volumes indicates the structure. The cultural centre De Flint in Amersfoort is a clear example of this, with the gently sloping pyramidic roof. In the Stadthalle of the South German Biberach an der Riss the structuralist principles have been more visibly applied by Greiner.

Diversity in the University

In the 1970s structuralism, in a series of university briefs in particular, was interpreted on a larger scale in extremely diverse ways. A colorful example of this is De Bastille for the University of Twente at Drienerlo. The building is only a part of the complex of buildings proposed by Piet Blom. On the exterior the building is completely faced with brick and inside is less simple to identify because of the mixture of the concrete skeleton with cores of brick and a great number of differences in level.

The department building for Applied Mathematics at Drienerlo, designed by Leo Heijdenrijk and Jos Mol, presents itself to the outside as being apparently extremely structuralist, but the skeleton is at various points concealed by concrete blocks. The prefabricated awnings of concrete components are not part of the actual construction, but do emphasise the articulation of the skeleton, as that became visible in the lower part of the building near ground level in particular. Within the building, as in De Bastille by Blom, there is an interweaving of the visible loadbearing construction and further filling in with concrete and brick. This makes the structuring construction less dominant.

A design on the boundary of structuralism is the Humanities Faculty on the Spuistraat in Amsterdam. In Theo Bosch's design the construction has remained visible everywhere, with the building up of departments around a central corridor and between them receding sections in the outer walls. However, there is less of a spatial structuring construction, while in the outer walls it is mainly the columns which have remained visible, particularly on the upper storeys.

The complex of the former Lerarenopleiding Zuidwest-Nederland in Delft, now in use by the Hogeschool Rotterdam and region, by Jan Tennekes, is an almost textbook example of structuralism. The configuration of cruciform towers which encloses interiors at some points, the unambiguous skeleton and the logical elaboration of the outer walls with between them the closed stairways have been designed in a very logical manner, but lack a more inventive interpretation of the rules of the game. Tennekes has also designed schools elsewhere on this pattern and used similar principles for hospitals in Purmerend and Almere, with a different building method.

Joop van Stigt designed two faculty buildings for the University of Leiden with between them the central university library by Bart van Kasteel. The three buildings have a combined cellar for parking, among other things. The skeleton construction is identical for the three buildings with striking mushroom-columns above the continuous underground cellar. Van Stigt used the pattern chosen for clusters of linked rectangles which together form an open urban fabric with inner courtyards and passageways accessible to the public. As opposed to these sixteen building sections with their own organization there is a single building volume for the library. The architectural detail also differs clearly for both architects. Joop van Stigt clearly reveals the striking columns in the outer walls and in use of materials and articulation links up with the existing environment. He demonstratively indicates the extendability by placing a number of columns on which there are only flower pots at the moment. Bart van Kasteel chose a construction which is only recognizable on the ground floor; above, the walls are finished with stone slabs and the mushroom columns in the outer wall area are transformed into round bays. In this way the library distinguishes itself from both faculty buildings.

Incitement to Utopias

The collective use of a single continuous construction system for a number of university buildings in Leiden seems to link up with utopian visions which proliferated both among artists and architects. It is the background to many structuralist designs. Already in the 1960s Constant (Nieuwenhuys) developed his New Babylon project, which after numerous exhibitions of elements was shown completely in the Haags Gemeentemuseum in 1974. Constant's fundamental principle in this was what he called 'Urbanisme unitaire'. In 1980 during a lecture at the University of Technology in Delft he explained this as follows: '...a complex and permanent activity with the aim of consciously changing the human environment in accordance with the most developed concepts in every field.' At another point Urbanisme unitaire is called the fruit of collective creativity of a completely different character. These two quotes from the declaration (Déclaration d/Amsterdam) are general enough for a broad interpretation and can still be used in relation to New Babylon.[33] Constant indicated here that, on the one hand, his built structures formed a reaction to the uniform postwar suburbs, and on the other hand were a taste of the future with a strongly increased degree of automation. Even then Constant was astonished by the growing structural unemployment, which meant, according to him, that people could no longer base their thinking on the utilitarian Charter of Athens, with the four functions based on work. He therefore developed a worldwide macrostructure which would offer people freedom of time and place: the continuity of a network instead of the quantity of separate settlements.[34]

Outside the Netherlands, it was mainly Yona Friedman who recorded similar ideas in drawings. In his 'Urban design sketch for New York' from 1964 Friedman shows a proposal for a spatial framework seven storeys high which is 12 metres above the ground and could cover a total of ten to twenty square kilometres.[35] In fact, the design shows a Utopian vision which was also at the root of Piet Blom's 'Urban roof'.

In England, six young architects united in the group Archigram.

Library, Doetinchem, 1976. Wim Davidse
Open space under a skylight in cruciform configuration

Faculty building Applied Mathematics and Computer Centre, University of Twente, Enschede, 1973. Leo Heijdenrijk and Jos Mol
Permanent external sunshades emphasise structuralist layout

Humanities faculty Amsterdam, 1984. Theo Bosch
Canal facade with strong articulation and in the foreground the Jugendstil building Het Witte Huis by J. Verheul, included in the complex

Faculty building and library, University of Leiden. Joop van Stigt and Bart van Kasteel
With Van Stigt mushroom-shaped columns for both buildings are for the most part on the exterior of the walls; Van Kasteel has positioned the columns on the first floor inside the outer walls

They developed various structures in which simple spatial cells could be placed. They showed themselves to be influenced by the new technology, as that was being developed for space travel among other things.[36]

On the other side of the world it was mainly the Japanese metabolists who were heard from after 1960. Led by CIAM and Team X member Kenzo Tange they also looked for structures in which simple spatial cells were included. Tange himself designed a new city for more than ten million inhabitants in Tokyo Bay, which in the course of time could grow, but even in different phases of growth would be a complete settlement. Like grids on top of each other were main roads, secondary roads and diverse structures for buildings for working, housing and leisure. This plan came into being around the CIAM congress in Otterlo in 1959 and was certainly discussed afterwards during the smaller meetings of Team X. In the Netherlands it led to the design of the 1965 Pampus plan by the architectural group Van den Broek and Bakema, with a linear urban extension in the Buiten-IJ, which however did not go as far in terms of structuralist design as did Kenzo Tange with Tokyo Bay.[37]

The plan however did incorporate experiences with housing groups from the Rotterdam extensions such as Pendrecht.

In 1969 Van den Broek and Bakema completed the Cityplan Eindhoven. For a demolition area in the centre of the city they developed an elongated high-rise. On a grid of 6 x 7.2 metres vertical traffic cores were fixed above an underground car park. During the planned phased building, in the course of time the space between the cores could be filled with the desired building height and so on.[38] The design was never built.

In this fashion, these more or less Utopian plans show that the characteristics of structuralism in the Netherlands were also in the ascendant elsewhere. Sometimes there is a clear mutual influence in the Team X context, as with Tange's Tokyo Bay and Van den Broek and Bakema's Pampusplan for the Buiten-IJ. But the built designs are smaller and show a more consciously desired interplay of functions.

Development of housing philosophies

The Forum idea had a great influence on social housing in the Netherlands. Piet Blom sought, in the words of Aldo van Eyck, new housing forms which were no longer based on the usual way of housing, nor on the narrow idea of what street, square, garden, room or door mean; nor on the rigid quartet of housing-work-leisure-traffic; nor on architecture and town planning as separate design activities. They were looking for a configurative radiation in which each dwelling possesses its own identity, something which in larger units with the correct connection leads to an enrichment of the housing environment. In a larger context these units would have to then make their identity possible in larger housing units. Therefore it was argued for a radical increase of the housing units, but only in a similar fugal process. With greater housing density more of an urban character would also become possible, with interwoven functions.

**New Babylon, 1971.
Constant (Nieuwenhuys)**
'View of New Babylon sectors', with a continuous network above city and country

Urban extension of Tokyo in Tokyo Bay, 1960. Kenzo Tange
Traffic and buildings were projected above the water in various grids

New Babylon, 1969
'Symbolic presentation' of a new structure above an existing landscape

New Babylon, 1972
'Entrance to a labyrinth'

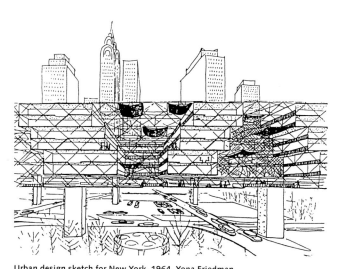

Urban design sketch for New York, 1964. Yona Friedman
A frame twelve metres above the ground in which new functions can be accommodated

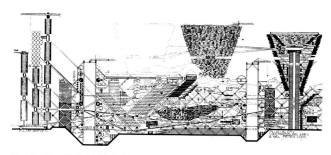

Plug-in City, 1964-1966. Archigram
The city as ongoing process of growth and change with the help of modern technology

Plan Pampus

In this manner many neighbourhoods were created with dwellings connected to each other to form many new configurations. They were expressed in new housing areas with a – sometimes almost endless – repetition of a single curved block, for example, or a 'cluster' consisting of a standard form of a few blocks. A representative example of this was the design by Henk Klunder for 1100 identical dwellings in uniform curved blocks of single-family dwellings for 'Europarkstad' in Leusden, of which only a part was built. The dwellings, shifted with regard to each other, had a sheltered exterior space with terrace and balcony as these were suggested with matchboxes in Forum. Residential districts were also built by people around the New Housing Forms Foundation, also ironically called the New Roof Forms Foundation, in Berkel en Rodenrijs, Den Helder, Rotterdam, Hoevelaken and Spijkenisse. Alongside the urban design configuration, extremely personal ideas about architecture and the desire for form led to picturesque details. The offshoots of this led to the snug housing architecture of the 1970s. The pursuit of expressive effect prevailed and was expressed in the details, which because of the limited budgets of social housing, were at the cost of the actual housing quality. This no longer had anything to do with structuralism.

In 1965 a different reaction came from a number of larger architectural bureaus, with the founding of the Architectural Research Foundation (SAR).[39] This was headed by N.J. Habraken who in 1961 in his book 'Supports and people' claimed that mass building of housing meant nothing more than 'prefabricated barracks-building'.[40]

The SAR aimed at a separation of loadbearing construction and interior walls, doors and the like. In this way the inhabitants would find it easier to give shape to their individual housing requirements, also with changing circumstances, such as more or fewer children in the home. In the development of the SAR methodology around 1965, new building was already taking possible changes and future renovations into account. Only the spaces such as kitchens, bathroom and toilets were fixed, along with the stairs, in the floor plan of the dwelling. In 1973 came a further development of the SAR philosophy in the publication 'The methodological formulation of agreements in designing fabrics'. A band grid was laid over future housing areas in which buildings and open spaces were indicated. In the margins within the grid space was included for any eventual later extension of the dwellings. Agreements about streets, blocks and other facilities were fixed to the extent that during the elaboration of building plans there would still be possibilities left for exceptions and shifts if they turned out to be necessary. In the De Batau extension in Nieuwegein Henk Reijenga and Jos Mol demonstrated the variable interpretation of the originally proposed urban structure and the freedom which the basic grid implied.

Although the SAR method linked up flawlessly with structuralism, in terms of its fundamental principles, the elaboration often remained traditionally rooted in the familiar shell shapes

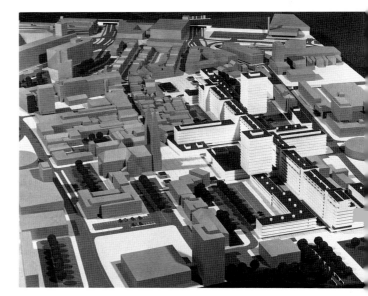

Cityplan Eindhoven, 1969. Van den Broek and Bakema
Construction, phased over time, of offices etc. between vertical shafts

Housing, Nieuwegein, 1980. Jan Verhoeven
Strong configuration around inner courts with a will to form reminiscent of the Amsterdam School

**Plan Pampus, Amsterdam, 1965.
Van den Broek and Bakema**
City extension in the Buiten-IJ, inspired by the plan by Kenzo Tange
for Tokyo Bay

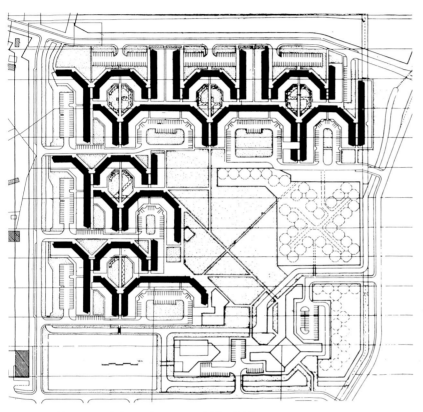

**Experimental housing, Berkel en Rodenrijs, 1973. Willem Brinkman,
Henk Klunder, Jan Verhoeven and Nico Witstok**
Configuration in the plan was incorrectly taken for structuralism

Housing Europarkstad, Leusden, 1972. Henk Klunder
Fragment of the entire plan for 1100 identical dwellings

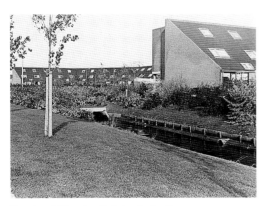

Experimental housing, Berkel en Rodenrijs

of traditional high-rise or concrete building. In these, the building walls which separated the dwellings frustrated the site topology of the dwellings within the block.

In Gouda-Bloemendaal the architectural bureau of De Jong, Van Olphen and Bax designed housing with an extra foundation joist outside the outer wall on which it was possible to increase the living space by building an extension or adding a conservatory.[41] However, these remained marginal possibilities as there was no skeleton.

Leo Heijdenrijk sought a housing structure which was constructed of standardised elements. His point of departure was a two-sided band grid of 2.4 by 3.6 metres. With the help of a skeleton the grid laid over the housing environment was filled in with dwellings of diverse sizes, whereby the standardization meant that as well as the possibility of the future inhabitants having a say in the size of the dwelling, there was also an immediate indication of the building costs. Apart from wet spaces and stairs, functions like living, sleeping, hobby room and the like were mutually interchangeable.

The same principles are to be found in Herman Hertzberger's diagoon dwellings, but the floors are placed split-level-style around a void in the centre of the dwelling. With the help of drawings of possible ways of filling it in, buyers could decide on further compartmentalisation of the open floor plan. On the ground floor the garage and portico could simply be changed in function and form. In the course of the years various inhabitants have used these possibilities in various ways. The diagoon dwellings can certainly be counted as being among the most structuralist dwellings in the Netherlands, alongside the dwellings of Bakema in the Eindhoven neighbourhood of 't Hool. The designs by Heijdenrijk were built in an altered form.

'Gründlich' structuralist housing

In Germany there was great interest for the SAR method developed in the Netherlands. This was applied on a large scale in Hamburg, where in designing blocks exchange of spaces between dwellings beside each other was taken into account. In this fashion it was hoped to achieve more flexible housing. Jos Weber supported the SAR method and argued for its use in Hamburg.

In Munich-Schwabbing in 1971 a housing project was built after a design by Otto Steidle & Partners, who established their bureau there, with architects Ralph and Doris Thut. Among the principles behind this exemplary structuralist design were interweaving of public and private areas around the dwelling entrances; there is also a pedestrian route under the block of dwellings. There was a very conscious search for flexible dwellings, individually and collectively, which were housed in a skeleton of reinforced concrete which remained visible, filled in with diverse building systems and materials from the suppliers' catalogues.

For the first block on the Genterstrasse seven bays were built varying in width from 5.75 to 7.55 metres. The skeleton con-

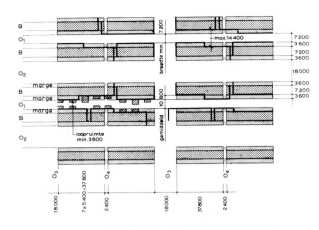

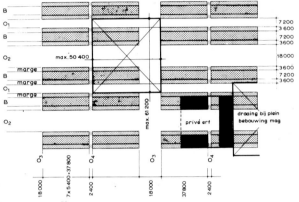

Town planning grid for Nieuwegein-De Batau, around 1974.
Henk Reijenga and Jos Mol
Possible layout of squares and residential streets

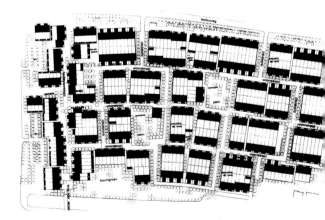

Nieuwegein-De Batau 1
Plan of the filled-in urban grid

Nieuwegein-De Batau
Cityscape with housing by Reijenga and Mol

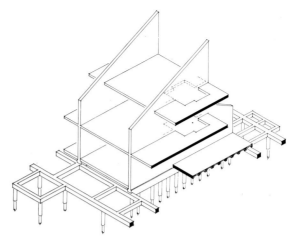

Dwellings Gouda-Bloemendaal, around 1974. De Jong, Van Olphen and Bax
Dwelling shell with extra joists for later extensions of the dwelling

Housing Gouda-Bloemendaal
Detail of the residential neighbourhood

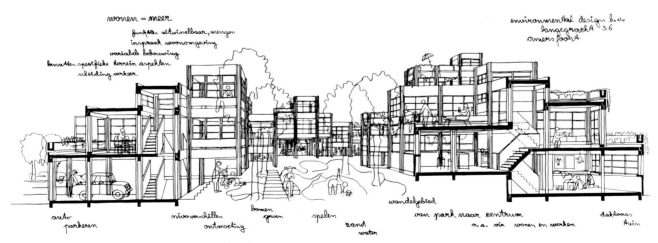

Study design, 'Housing is more', around 1974. Leo Heijdenrijk
Differentiated housing with the aid of a building system with prefabricated concrete

sists of prefabricated standard columns with consoles for placing beams on. The building system which the skeleton is derived from was often used for production sheds and the like and had consoles at half-storey height. According to the wishes of the inhabitants, rooms of both one and one-and-a-half stories high could be included. Because the columns continued on for another storey above the roof, extension could easily take place. Balconies and terraces within the skeleton also made enlargement of the housing area of the dwelling possible by shifting glass walls. For the layout of stairs and wet spaces zones were applied which are related to the SAR method and according to Kenneth Frampton mesh with the ideas of Habraken.[42]

Diagoon dwellings, Delft-Buitenhof, 1971. Herman Hertzberger

Such a logical form of structuralism in the building of housing has never been so 'gründlich' designed and built in the Netherlands. Steidle further developed the dwellings for an entry for the big 1972 German housing competition Elementa for Nürnberg. In this he used the SAR method in a competition design which was then built. He also realised more experiments around the Genterstrasse in Munich.[43]

Around 1970 a competition 'Wohnen Morgen' was set in each region of Austria with the goal of realising future-oriented experiments. Ottokar Uhl won the first prize for a project in Hollabrun in Niederösterreich.[44] Because it was an Austrian competition, the assistance of Jos Weber and the SAR method was not mentioned. Uhl later said that he regarded the SAR method as opening up new horizons for humane housing and had chosen this method after comparing it with numerous similar developments in Europe.

The blocks were built with a bay width of 5.1 metres. In the block depth, a construction zone of 2.4 metres wide round columns were alternated with 7.2 x 7.2 metres arches, on a bay width of 1.2 metres. In this, diverse dwelling types were built across one or two bays and with one or two floors, reached from an inner street with stairs to the upper dwellings. Here too the skeleton of round columns with beams between them was continued outside the walls in order to make it easy to extend the dwellings at a later date. Within the dwellings the walls are moveable if needed.

The design has direct connections, in terms of its layout, with Dutch structuralism, although via the roundabout route of the SAR method and Jos Weber, who worked in Hamburg. The project demonstrates that the design principles of the Dutch structuralists had an effect outside the Netherlands in the 1970s. Because of the strong emphasis on standardization of prefabricated elements, the architecture is somewhat crude.

Dwellings in Munich-Schwabing, 1971. Otto Steidle with Ralph and Doris Thut
The skeleton continued outside the dwelling makes it simple to expand in the future

International interactions

After the term structuralism emerged in 1973 in Dutch articles and speech,[46] it was the correspondent of the journal Bauen+Wohnen, Arnulf Lüchinger, who was studying in Delft, who compiled a theme number on structuralism as a new movement in architecture[47], through which the name became

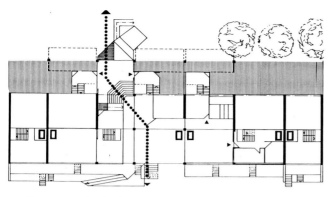

Dwellings in Munich-Schwabing
Floor plan with pedestrian route under the dwellings

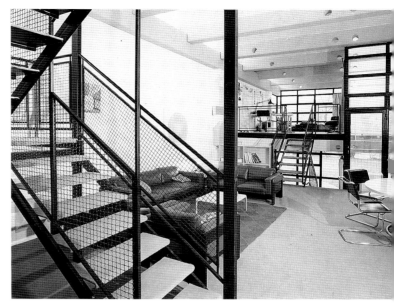

Dwellings in Munich-Schwabing
Interior with split-level floors

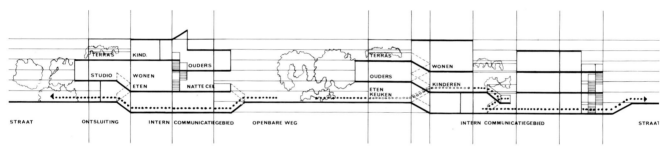

Dwellings in Munich-Schwabing
Cross section in first and second building phase

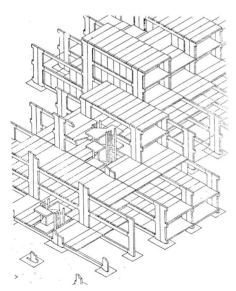

**'Wohnen Morgen', Hollabrun, 1976.
Ottokar Uhl and Jos Weber**
Structural layout in prefabricated concrete

'Wohnen Morgen', Hollabrun
The dwellings can be extended between the skeleton

internationally known and was taken up. Characteristic of the linguistic confusion of the time was that as well as structuralist works such as De Drie Hoven in Amsterdam, Muziekcentrum Vredenburg in Utrecht and the chapel for Kerk en Wereld in Driebergen, all kinds of configurative designs were documented, such as housing in Leusden and Berkel en Rodenrijs. Although these projects showed points of contact with the Forum idea, they were definitely not structuralist.

Lüchinger also pointed out diverse relations with the work of internationally famous architects. For example, in 1925 Le Corbusier had already designed student housing where blocks from a grid were filled in with student rooms on corridors with individual roof terraces. Although an aerial view suggests a relationship with the roofscapes of Blom's Kasbah, the French design bears no relation to structuralism. That was indeed the case with Le Corbusier's design for the hospital in Venice. The design in four storeys is partly built above the water as in the town hall design by Heijdenrijk for Amsterdam. The various storeys in Venice are laid over each other as divergent grids and filled in in ways which link up with the diverse functions around vertical ascension points and the structuring construction. The design from 1965 was never built.

Related ideas can also be found in Louis Kahn who in 1955 had already remarked that '...designing is giving form to organization, form is born from a construction system, growth is a structure. A creative power is hidden in organising, in designing the means – where, with what, when, with how much? In the essence of the space is reflected what it wants to be.'[48] As examples of Kahn's work, Arnulf Lüchinger named in Bauen+Wohnen the design for the Jewish community centre in Trenton (N.Y.) from 1954 and the Richards Medical Research Building in Philadelphia from 1961. In both designs the space-structuring construction is to be found, in the same way as it forms the basis of structuralism. The Research Building in particular with square towers and between them the cores for vertical traffic and wiring shafts showed affinities with Hertzberger's layout for Centraal Beheer. The American design was shown and elucidated by Kahn at the CIAM congress in Otterlo.[49]

Lüchinger also mentioned the press centre in Kofu designed by Kenzo Tange in 1967 and the 1960 design for Tokyo Bay. As in other plans by Tange vertical cores play a dominant role here, with between them fillings which link up with the programme of requirements and sometimes leave a lot open at certain points, as in the press centre. Tange himself has described his transition from a functional to a more structuralist architecture in 'Funktion, Struktur und Symbol'[50]. In this he claimed that after 1960 the separation of functions, also in specific spaces, no longer fitted in a time in which flexibility was becoming increasingly important.

It became clear that in the work of leading CIAM members such as Le Corbusier, and Team X participants like Louis Kahn and Kenzo Tange, interactions in their architecture had taken place because of their contacts with each other. In a number of countries such as Germany and Denmark that has led to a number of structuralist works, but nowhere has it been as versatilely and logically developed as in the Netherlands.

It is notable what Lüchinger wrote about the affinities of the emerging structuralism with the research in the human sciences being done simultaneously by the French scholar Claude Lévi-Strauss. He claimed that for each language a number of phonemes are selected which make it possible to put thought into words. Sounds and rules form a structure in the languages which also occurs in the forms of society. His research showed that the so-called primitive cultures were essentially no different than the modern Western forms of society. Dutch architects were to feel a great affinity with this theory, according to Arnulf Lüchinger in his later book on structuralism.[51] In his courses at the Technical University in Delft Herman Hertzberger indicated that structuralism in the 1960s did indeed come to the fore with the cultural anthropology in Paris, and he then mentioned ideas about the relation of collective pattern and individual interpretation of it as being of interest and exceptionally inspiring for architecture.[52] But comparisons can be found just as often with music or chess, in which the individual choice of the rules of the game can lead to an individual wealth of expression.

European developments
The developments within Dutch structuralism are sometimes parallel to European work by architects associated with Team X. For example, Georges Candilis has said that in the twenty years after the war more was built than in the thousand years that preceded it. Dissatisfied, he claimed: 'People are building modern, but what does that mean! From a serious discussion of fundamental problems of principle in the 1930s architecture slipped into an absurd formalism.'[53] This dissatisfaction was expressed in a competition design for the Römer in Frankfurt am Main between town hall and cathedral. With Alexis Josic and Shadrach Woods, Candilis developed a flexible structure in which generations could develop further. The professional jury threw out the plan, but Candilis was pleased to point out that the younger generation had received the plan enthusiastically and in this way had taken the right road at the beginning of the 1960s.[54]

A similar design for the competition for the University in Bochum met the same fate, but in Berlin they hit the bull's eye. As foreign architects they has also been invited for this German competition and they developed an urban fabric a number of storeys high. All the spaces for education, research and administration were located on freely accessible inner streets with secondary routes crossing them at right angles as in a grid, around green patios. The first phase of the competition design from 1962 was built between 1967 and 1972. The flexibility has been efficiently woven into the design; with the Berlin architect Manfred Schiedhelm a construction of steel and prefabricated concrete was developed in which wiring could also

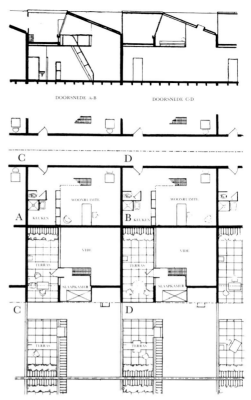

DOORSNEDE A-B   DOORSNEDE C-D

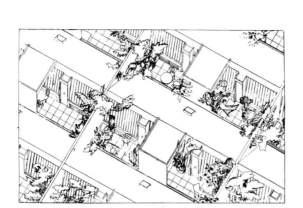

Student housing, 1925. Le Corbusier
Aerial view with roof terraces

Student housing
Cross section and floor plans

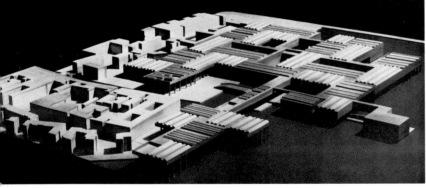
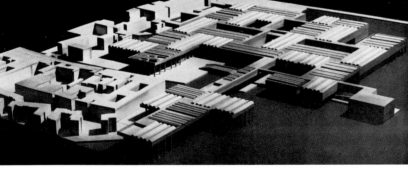

Design of hospital for Venice, 1965. Le Corbusier
The hospital for 1200 beds had entrances, administration and kitchen on the ground floor, operating theatres and nurses' rooms on the first floor, on the second floor the central connections and on the third floor the beds

Richards Medical Research Building, Philadelphia, 1961. Louis Kahn
Separation of work towers and vertical shafts for lifts, stairs and wiring

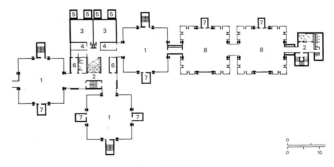

Richards Medical Research Building, Philadelphia
Schematic floor plan
1   studio towers
2   elevators and stairways
3   animal quarters
4   animal service rooms
5   fresh air intake shafts
6   air distribution shafts
7   fume and exhaust shafts
8   biology laboratory towers

be simply included. The walls were designed as sandwich elements of steel in cooperation with the Frenchman Jean Prouvé. The elements were mutually interchangeable in the outer wall, as internal use of space made this desirable. The construction was inside the walls and was simply manipulated for bigger spaces. Originally, weather-proof (corten) steel was used for the walls, but they changed over to aluminium later, in the second building phase. Remarkably enough, a foreigner also got the second prize in the Berlin competition. Because of the admiration for his structuralist competition design, the Dane Henning Larsen was commissioned to design the nearby building for the Department of Physics. The complex which was built between 1976 and 1981 is also based on a grid and seems to be somewhat cleaner in layout and detail.

Candilis's Berlin design made a deep impression on the Danish architects Knud Holscher, Kron & Hartvig Rasmussen Ass.. A publication of the design inspired their design for the University of Odense. In the park-like landscape of a suburb a grid was laid down, reached by a central traffic axis and class rooms around courtyards. The design was built almost simultaneously with the Berlin plan, between 1970 and 1973.

The great Scandinavian interest in structuralism was also expressed in a Swedish/Danish publication.[55] In this the then editor of 'Arkitektur DK', Poul-Erik Skriver, placed the discussion of the structure in the office building for Norske Veritas by Lund and Slaatos next to Hertzberger's design for Centraal Beheer. It was a completely individual development of the idea which was certainly influenced by Centraal Beheer, and may even have originated in it. That is also true of the head offices of the Finnish dairy giant Valio. The complex of separate square office buildings around core spaces two storeys high was designed by Matti K. Mäkinen after he had studied the design of Centraal Beheer, but he too developed the structuralist principles in an individual manner.[56]

In 1967 the Swedish architect Rolf Rickard Thies won the competition for the design of a town hall for Malmö. On a foundation with car park a big hall-like space was envisaged in which office floors of around 25 by 30 metres were placed split-level-style with wide voids between them. The jury emphasised the importance of this winning design by not awarding any second prize, but two third prizes.[57] Nevertheless, the promising design was never built. It would have been a remarkable expression of structuralism, through the clear manner in which the construction of office floors was perceivable in an equally structured main space.

The Bagsværd church by Jørn Utzon from 1976 was also associated by Poul-Erik Skriver with structuralism[58], which is debatable. Utzon's design for the furniture company Paustian in the harbour district of Copenhagen however, has all the characteristics of structuralism. For the building, built between 1985 and 1987, Jørn Utzon used prefabricated elements of concrete for the skeleton and floors. This remained completely visible as space-structuring construction. The outer walls have clearly

been treated as skeleton fillers and inside the building voids provide visual contact between the various departments.

The most fascinating example of structuralism in Denmark however, is to be found in the Kunstmuseum of Holstebro in North Jutland. The first phase of the design by Hanne Kjærholm was completed in 1981, the second phase was completed in 1990. In its main lines, the design seems to be influenced by the internationally acclaimed Louisiana museum in Humlebæk by Jørgen Bo and Vilhelm Wohlert. The execution however, points to an influence of the Utrecht Muziekcentrum Vredenburg by Herman Hertzberger. The new building behind an existing villa consists alternately of a band grid of around 6 x 6 metres with between them light shafts around 2 metres wide. At some places this pattern has been deviated from with two broad bays alongside each other.

With a slight constriction, the round columns of the concrete skeleton turn into the end beams of the grid of beams of the coffer floor of the roof. The light shafts between the flat roofs have a semi-circular ending which in some places turns into glass walls. The skeleton has been freely manipulated to the extent that the roof floors rest on brick walls where possible, as is also the case with Aldo van Eyck's Burgerweeshuis. The glass walls have been here logically placed within the columns; when the glass walls are here and there almost under the eaves, these are curved onwards at the columns. If Hertzberger has glass and brickwork link up logically in as many ways as possible with the round columns, Hanne Kjærholm also manipulates the glass walls logically around the columns, but retains an association with the foyers of Vredenburg. With the limited repertoire of columns, closed walls of brickwork and glass, she achieves a richly varied alternation of spaces, in terms of layout comparable with the Burgerweeshuis of Aldo van Eyck, who needed just as few different building elements.

Scale enlargement in the 1980s

In the 1980s the face of structuralism in the Netherlands was above all determined by larger building tasks. The university buildings in Leiden and Amsterdam are examples which have already been mentioned. Remarkable was the detail, tending almost to postmodernism, in the masonry of the walls of the faculty buildings which Joop van Stigt designed in Leiden. A similar picturesque approach can be found, intensified, in the Fire Brigade Academy in Schaarsbergen by Jan Verhoeven. His work is almost always dominated by a strong desire for configuration in relation to a very expressive use of detail in the brickwork, which is reminiscent of the Amsterdam School, but built in a less colourful manner. In the Schaarsbergen complex the small-scale of the 1970s predominates. The detail is often illogical such as roof tiles for vertical wall sections and amazingly manipulated drainpipes for rainwater which conflict directly with sound engineering details.[59]

The same use of typical Dutch building materials such as brick and ceramic roof tiles is found in the building for the Social

**Freie Universität, Geistes Wissenschaft, Berlin, 1972.
Candilis, Josic and Woods with Schiedhelm**
First phase with interchangeable wall segments developed
together with Jean Prouvé

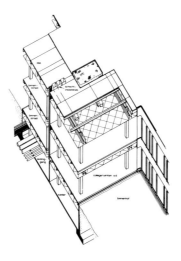

Freie Universität Berlin
Steel construction with
'stacked' sections and wiring
between them

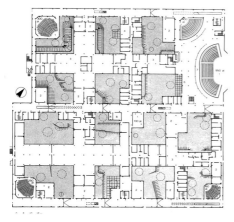

Freie Universität Berlin
Floor plan of the first phase

Freie Universität Berlin, Physikalische Institut, 1981. Henning Larsen
Inner court with classrooms around it

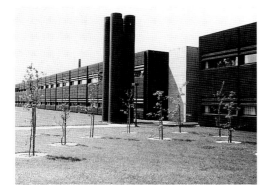

**Odense Universitet, 1971.
Knud Holscher of Krohn and Hartvig Rasmussen**
End wall with weather-resistant steel

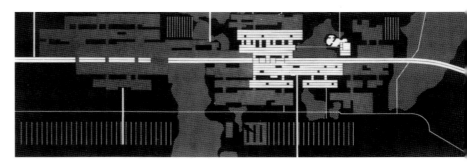

Odense Universitet
Main structure with first building phase in white

Head offices Norske Veritas
Floor plan office storey

Head offices Norske Veritas, Høvik. Lund and Slaatos
The new building on the water

Head offices Valio, Helsinki
Interior around a two-storey high central space

Head offices Valio, Helsinki, 1978. Matti K. Mäkinen and Kaarina Löfström

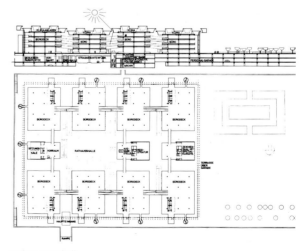

Malmö town hall
Floor plan and cross section

Malmö town hall, 1967. Rolf Rickard Thies
The open interior around office floors

Showroom of Paustian furniture, Copenhagen, 1987. Jørn Utzon
Interior around the central void

Holstebro Museum of Art
Museum space

Holstebro Museum of Art, 1981 and 1990. Hanne Kjærholm
Exterior first phase

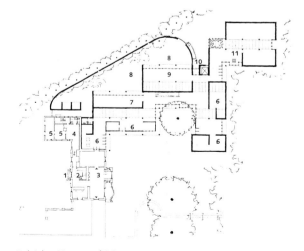

Holstebro Museum of Art
Floor plan. 1 to 5 existing villa, 6 to 11 new building first phase 1981

Services in Leeuwarden by Abe Bonnema. The building was already completed in 1975 and shows a clear desire to fit in with the architecture of the existing environment. This was less necessary at the rear, and splendid flat roofs with flower pots were created.

The staff of the Provinciaal Elektriciteitsbedrijf Noord-Holland (PEN) had a say in the choice of architect for the new company building along the boundary of Alkmaar. They visited the Centraal Beheer and the Social Services in Leeuwarden and then chose Bonnema as architect. Impressed by the roof gardens in Leeuwarden, in Alkmaar they requested roof terraces which could also make it possible to step outside for a moment on the first floor. Abe Bonnema complied by giving a completely individual expression to the clearly structuralist design of the complex at the edge of the North Holland landscape. The desired energy-saving layout had far-reaching consequences for the skeleton visible in the outer walls. By pouring strips of insulating material into the corner columns behind the reinforcement, condensation on the column which ran from outside to inside was avoided.

In the Ministry of Foreign Affairs in The Hague by Dick Apon, which has affinities with structuralism, the columns with an octagonal cross section are placed completely outside the wall. In order to avoid cold conductors, insulation material and prefabricated concrete scales have been placed around the columns, which meant that the columns which were originally 75 centimetres in diameter became 90 centimetres.[60]

In the Ministry of Education and Science by Flip Rosdorff, built at the same time, the dilemma of the cold conductor led to a change of principle in the architecture, with the structuralist idea being maintained. The concrete skeleton remained visible within the building, on the exterior a curtain wall was placed in which the position of the columns and walls was carefully indicated. In fact, this solutions refers back to the university walls in Berlin and Odense, where the wall elements of the two Danish designs in their dimensions link up more directly with the arches of the construction in the skeleton.

Similar developments were also to be seen in the building of a number of teaching hospitals. The complex installations with great numbers of wires and the necessary flexibility in connection with constant changes in the medical techniques made it necessary to have a structuralist main layout in the design. A typical example of this is the Amsterdam Medical Centre in Amsterdam-Zuidoost. The architecture of the outer walls is comparable to that of an industrial building and not structuralist. Within the walls however, you can find a grid of inner streets with blocks in which are housed treatment departments, labs, university facilities and administrative departments. Here, the building became a small city with high spatial quality within the building's skin and it shows affinities with the design for the town hall of Malmö by Rolf Rickard Thies, except here the spaces on the inner streets are given interior facades. Similar principles can be found in other academic hospitals, often

based on foreign examples such as the hospital of MC Master University in Ontario by Eberhard Zeidler.[61]

In the design for the Ministry of Social Affairs and Employment in The Hague which was for the most part designed and built in the 1980s, Herman Hertzberger stayed faithful to a construction with towers, but he thoroughly altered the configuration. The towers are now clustered orthogonally around central inner courts and the main construction has the diagonal as its main direction. Because the users were of the opinion that they could not do their work in rooms on conservatory-like inner courts, a very expressive wall structure came into being with the greatest possible length in order to be able to situate as many work spaces as possible on the outer walls. The rooms on the high inner courts are now mainly used as conference rooms and the like. In the preliminary design the high inner street covered the entire length of the building as central access to all the office towers. But in the built design too, the high conservatories with coffee corners were retained as spaces in which the desire for social exchange and collegial contacts was just as insistently present as in the voids of Centraal Beheer.

Under pressure from the client, the Government Buildings Department, the number of columns in the walls was strictly minimalised for the benefit of aluminium curtain walls and infills of masonry in concrete blocks. But at various points high glass walls have been applied for the conservatories and the secondary stairs.

Discussions

In the 1980s in the Netherlands a structuralist architect needed a lot of stamina in order to keep his architectural ideas afloat, in the face of a too one-sided emphasis on engineering conditions, which can easily become an end in themselves. It sometimes also formed a stimulus to discussions of whether structuralism was still viable and to what extent buildings had to be ascribed to structuralism. A salient discussion took place in the yearbooks of the Dutch Architectural Institute. In 1989 Hans van Dijk announced the premature demise of structuralism, claiming that the vital renewal around the beginning of the 1960s would be missing in the late 1980s.[62] A year later Joseph Buch fervently contested this view in the next number of the same yearbook.[63] He argued that as a foreigner he had 'discovered' Dutch structuralism: 'Here were buildings which really looked like buildings...and in lowrise! We were also crazy about them because they looked so Dutch – more Dutch than anything since De Klerk. Without looking for a national style the Dutch architects in the 1970s had succeeded in making something unique and regional more than the consciously nationalist Delft School.'[64] In the same article Buch announced that structuralism was taught as a main subject at the University of Auckland, New Zealand, showing that worldwide there is more than historical interest in structuralism. Buch is not alone in this, and the interest exists on the international stage too. The editor of the Architectural Review from London, Peter Buchanan,

Fire Brigade Academy, Schaarsbergen, 1981. Jan Verhoeven
Picturesque configuration under a complicated roofscape with red tiles

PEN offices, Alkmaar, 1982. Abe Bonnema
Central inner court with water

Ministry of Foreign Affairs, The Hague, 1984. D.C. Apon
The skeleton is covered with insulating material and finished in prefabricated concrete

noted that many architects in the Netherlands at the end of the 1980s had lost their way in their design practice and advised the designers not to allow themselves to be seduced by trendy internationalism, but to once again update structuralism for renewed use.[65]

Two other factors play an important role. Again and again the question arises which Jürgen Joedicke had already asked at an early stage: when can a building be ascribed to structuralism? Buildings often do not meet all the characteristics which are mentioned here and it is up the viewer to say whether the building is structuralist or not.

A striking example of this is the building for the Rijksdienst voor het Oudheidkundig Bodemonderzoek in Amersfoort by Abel Cahen. The building was designed in the tradition of the Forum idea, but lacks the structuring construction because of the traditional construction of brick outer and inner walls with floor constructions included in them. A number of prefabricated window surrounds and columns between window frames do look structuralist but are only part of the outer walls, without having any further relation with the actual construction of the building.

There are also the less successful examples of structuralism. In 1980, Rem Koolhaas was already complaining: 'From the first "family" units of Van Eyck, via Hertzberger's celebrated subdivided offices for Centraal Beheer, this model has been exhausted and debased, reaching a phase of extreme decadence where it has become responsible for an acute crisis of legibility, now that orphanages, student homes, housing, offices, prisons, department stores, concert halls, all look the same.'[67] That was somewhat one-sided a view, but naturally there have been forms of simplified imitation which Hertzberger has characterised as 'Chinese Puzzles'.

New impetus

At the end of the 1980s structuralism in the Netherlands received a number of powerful impulses. Herman Hertzberger was invited to participate in important foreign competitions. For the altered completion of a large museum complex on the Berlin Kulturforum, for which Rolf Gutbrod originally made the design, Hertzberger designed a Gemäldegalerie. In this design, strongly divergent layouts for different floors were once again laid over each other. The actual museum for paintings was given a fascinating construction with an entirely new museum landscape. Visitors could make both a chronological circuit along the paintings, or deviate from this by using cross connections. The exhibition walls were flexible in design and offered not only diverse possibilities for exhibiting paintings against suitable backgrounds, but could also be replaced by glass cases if required by changing exhibitions policy. The access of daylight through the roof construction was combined with a series of installation corridors which could also serve as transport routes for paintings from the store. Although the site had limitations, with the partly realised complex of Gut-

brod and the preservation of two pre-war dwellings, realization would have led to an extremely visitor-friendly museum and would have added a new dimension to structuralism.[68]

For the competition for the Bibliothèque de France in Paris too, Hertzberger developed an extremely structuralist design, which was not built either. On a base partly sunk into the site a main structure of round columns was envisaged with two to three very high floors, as in the painting stores in the Berlin museum design. In this main structure Hertzberger designed building volumes which were placed as containers, as sub-library units. In both examples very large interiors were created, a new element within Dutch structuralism. They showed once again that Hertzberger had no objection to big building volumes, when they once again acquire a human scale when further developed.

A completely different impulse was the building of an extension for Estec in Noordwijk after a design by Aldo and Hannie van Eyck. On the edge of the dunes and former meadow landscape the office building was built with a facilities centre consisting of a restaurant, library and conference accommodation. The office is constructed of linked towers which show an affinity with the office buildings of Hertzberger. The Van Eycks manipulated the square floor plan by bevelling off the corners and turning the sides inward into an almost organic whole. The choice for untreated hardwood for the outer walls was daring in a maritime climate but links up extremely well with the adjoining dune landscape. The wall sections of iroko, each one storey high, are stacked protruding slightly outward, as also happened in the Netherlands in the middle ages.

In the facilities centre the Van Eycks developed a completely new concept in structuralism, using the segments of a circle. The circle already played an important role in the Sonsbeek pavilion, the design for the chapel in Driebergen and various exhibition designs. For the restaurant a configuration was developed, built up of ring-shaped building volumes or segments of them, with bays which enrich the configuration. The roof surfaces which slope towards the edges are crowned in the middle by expressively designed skylights. The steel construction is quite unique and is distinguished by a logical construction of light, single columns in the wall area to joined main columns under the space-structuring roof construction. The constructive structure is reminiscent of early steel constructions for greenhouses and exhibition buildings.

The alternation of larger and smaller rooms, which run into each other in a complex bunch, lends a new dimension to the Forum idea. The spectral use of colour in Aldo van Eyck's favorite colours (the rainbow) for steel construction and a collection of diverse classic and recent Thonet seats emphasise the spatial form created.

In 1991 Herman Hertzberger won a multiple commission for a block of the Media-Park in Cologne. The configuration with curved office buildings links up with the up-to-date nature of the Estec facilities centre which had been completed shortly be-

Ministry of Social Affairs and Employment, The Hague, 1990.
Herman Hertzberger

**Estec facilities centre,
Noordwijk, 1980, Aldo
and Hannie van Eyck**
The space-structuring
construction is within
the outer walls and roof

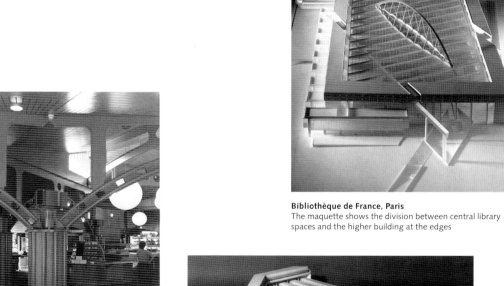

Bibliothèque de France, Paris
The maquette shows the division between central library
spaces and the higher building at the edges

Gemäldegalerie, Berlin, 1986. Herman Hertzberger
The maquette shows the division between the museum space with
upper corridors for transporting paintings, skylights between them
and a higher building at the edge for museum storage

fore. Hertzberger himself referred mainly to the Sonsbeek pavilion with the contracted corridors between curved walls. The way in which the semi-circular interiors can be used for studios which can be changed over time and other big spaces once again recalls the visionary sketches of Yona Friedman and Constant.

Each of these recent designs has been innovative within Dutch structuralism; they form unexpected impulses for structuralism as a living architectural school in the 1990s. Now that there is much interest among younger architects in recent architectural schools, such as the Nieuwe Bouwen and the postwar reactions to it, structuralism can form an intriguing example of what Buchanan meant by the examination of existing designs, in order to rework them in a personal style and in doing so make new contributions to the specific Dutch architectural tradition.

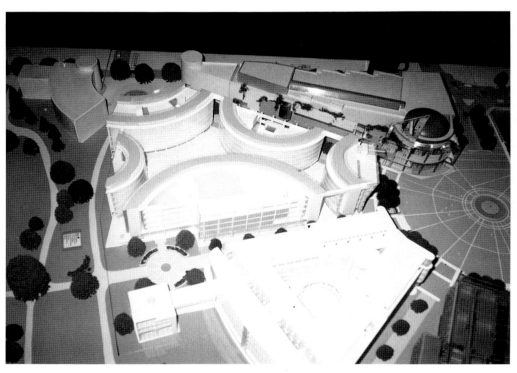

Media-Park, Cologne, 1991. Herman Hertzberger
In the configuration of curved blocks the curved facade on the square formed a structural starting-point

Notes

1 Auke van der Woud: 'Het Nieuwe Bouwen Internationaal/International CIAM Volkshuisvesting Stedebouw/Housing Town Planning', Otterlo/Delft, 1983, pp 102
2 See note 1, pp 102
3 Oscar Newman: 'CIAM '59 in Otterlo', Hilversum/Stuttgart, 1961
4 Jaap Bakema: 'Samenhang tussen mensen en dingen', Forum 1952 no 6/7 pp 170–171
5 See note 1
6 Joop Hardy and Herman Hertzberger: 'Drempel en ontmoeting: de gestalte van het tussen', Forum 1959 no 8 pp 249–278
7 Forum (Maandblad voor architectuur en gebonden kunsten) 1959 no 7 to 1963 no 3, and a supplementary number in July 1967, published as 1963 no 4. The monthly appeared irregularly
8 Forum 1959 no 9 pp 285–309: '5 projecten', 1960 no 1: '5 projecten', 1960/61 no 5 pp 159–188: 'Het andere wonen', 1960/61 no 8 pp 253–284: 'Het andere wonen', 1962 no 5 pp 171–216: 'Het andere wonen'
9 Jaap Bakema: 'Een huis in Spangen voor 270 families', Forum 1960/61 no 5 pp 159–170
10 Jaap Bakema: 'Schindler's spel met de ruimte', Forum 1960/61 no 8 pp 253–263
11 Alison and Peter Smithson: 'Geterrasseerde wooneenheden', Forum 1959 no 9 pp 304–309
12 Ralph Erskine: 'Poolstad project', Forum 1960/61 no 1 pp 2–7
13 Moshe Safdie: 'Fallacies, nostalgia and reality' and 'A case for city living', Forum 1962 no 5 pp 171–184
14 Jaap Bakema: 'Plan Kennemerland', Forum 1960/61 no 1 pp 28–35
15 Jaap Bakema: 'Bouwen voor de anonieme opdrachtgever', Forum 1962 no 2 pp 70–74
16 Aldo van Eyck: 'De verkapte opdrachtgever en het grote woord neen', Forum 1962 no 3 pp 79–122
17 Wim F. van Bodegraven quoted in the Forum CIAM number, 1952 no 6/7 pp 171 and Forum 1959 no 7 pp 216
18 Aldo van Eyck: 'De milde raderen van de reciprociteit – Kindertehuis in Amsterdam', Forum 1961 no 6/7 pp 195–235
19 See note 18
20 Letter from Rietveld to Aldo van Eyck of 27 November 1960, published in facsimile in architectuur/bouwen 1987 no 5 pp 29
21 Jürgen Joedicke: 'Architektur Geschichte des 20. Jahrhunderts', Stuttgart, 1990
22 Joop van Stigt: 'Eindkamp voor de Prix de Rome 1962', commentary on the design, Forum 1963 no 1 pp 4–20
23 Dick Apon: 'Een dorp als een huis, een dorp voor kinderen', Forum 1963 no 1 pp 21–24
24 Invited were the architects D.C. Apon, J.L.C. Choisy, G.J. van der Grinten, H. Hertzberger and A. van Kranendonk. The competition is exhaustively documented in TABK 1967 no 4 pp 73–91 and no 5 pp 97–120
25 Herman Hertzberger: 'Het glazen slot', Katholiek Bouwblad 1961 no 5 pp 96–105
26 The editors (by now different) devoted an 'extra' number to it, Forum 1969 no 4 pp 1–27
27 'a/b gesprek' Herman Hertzberger with Jan Benthem and Mels Crouwel, architectuur/bouwen 1985 no 9 pp 33–37
28 Herman Hertzberger: 'Ruimte maken – ruimte laten', Delft, 1984 and 'Lessons for students in architecture', Rotterdam, 1991
29 See note 27
30 Herman Hertzberger: 'Huiswerk voor meer herbergzame vorm', Forum 1973 no 3
31 'Study for an urban grid', commentary on a study plan for the Amsterdam School of Architecture, Higher Architectural Course, TABK 1968 no 17 pp 410–430
32 Announcement of the ideas competition on Church-building set by the editors of TABK and the Interdiocesan committee for church-building, TABK 1968 no 3 (announcement of the competition) and no 19 and 24 (results of the competition)
33 Constant (Nieuwenhuys): 'New Babylon na tien jaren', lecture on 23 May 1980, Architectural Department TU Delft, Delft, 1980
34 J.L. Locher and Constant (Nieuwenhuys): 'New Babylon', exhibition catalogue Municipal Museum of The Hague, 1974
35 J. Trapman: 'Principiële mogelijkheden van de flexibiliteit in de woningbouw, nieuwe lettertekens voor de taal van de stedebouw', Forum 1964 no 4 pp 1–39
36 Peter Cook: 'Archigram', London, 1972 and Basle, 1972 and 1991
37 Architectural group Van den Broek & Bakema: 'Architektur – Urbanismus / Architecture-Urbanism / Architecture-Urbanisme', Stuttgart, 1975 pp 24–29
38 'City plan Eindhoven', exhibition catalogue Van Abbemuseum, Eindhoven, s.a. (±1969)
39 Participating in the Stichting Architecten Research were the Bond van Nederlandse Architecten and the architectural bureaus E.F. Groosman, F. Klein, Kraaijvanger, Lucas and Niemeijer, Maaskant, Van Dommelen, Kroos and Senf, Zanstra, Gmelig Meijling and De Clercq Zubli and J. P. Kloos
40 John Habraken: 'De dragers en de mensen', Haarlem, 1961 and 1972
41 Wim J. van Heuvel: 'Experimentele woningbouw – verkenning van gerealiseerde werken', The Hague, 1976 pp 58–59
42 Kenneth Frampton: 'Modern architecture and the critical present, London, 1982 pp 62
43 Otto Steidle and Gerhard Ullmann: 'Stadthäuser aus industriell hergestellten Teilen', Deutsche Bauzeitung 1980 no 1 pp 9–16
44 'Wohnen Morgen – Baukünstlerischer Wettbewerb Niederösterreich' edited by Kurt Heiduk, Vienna, s.a. (±1972)
45 Jos Weber and Ottokar Uhl: 'Dwellings in a realised SAR-support' part 1 'Background' and part 2 'Dwelling forms', Delft/Karlsruhe, s.a.
46 Arnaud Beerends: 'Valkenswaard – Amsterdam – Apeldoorn: een hink-stap-sprong van Herman Hertzberger', Wonen/TABK 1973 no 5 pp 9–21. Beerends used the word structuralism here, after having previously only written about the structure of Hertzberger's town halls
47 Arnulf Lüchinger: 'Strukturalismus – eine neue Strömung in der Architektur', special issue Bauen+Wohnen 1976 no 1
48 From 'Perspecta' 1955 no 3; quoted by Romaldo Giurgola and Jaimini: 'Louis Kahn – Architect', Zürich, 1975
49 Oscar Newman: 'CIAM '59 in Otterlo', Stuttgart/Hilversum, 1961 pp 205–216
50 Kenzo Tange: 'Funktion, Struktur und Symbol 1966', Zürich, 1970
51 Arnulf Lüchinger: 'Strukturalismus in Architektur und Städtebau/Structuralism in Architecture and Urban Planning/Structuralisme en architecture et urbanisme', Stuttgart, 1981
52 See note 28
53 Georges Candilis: 'Bauen ist Leben – ein Architekten Report', Stuttgart, 1978
54 See note 53
55 Anders Ekholm, Nils Ahrbom, Peter Broberg and Poul-Erik Skriver: 'Utvecklingen mot Strukturalism i Arkitekturen', Stockholm, 1980
56 On a tour in July 1980, Matti Mäkinen pointed out this influence to me
57 Wim J. van Heuvel: 'Nieuwe architectuurontwikkelingen in Malmö', Cobouw 2 May 1975 with source Bauwelt 1975 no 27
58 Poul-Erik Skriver: 'Bagsværd Kirke', Arkitektur DK 1982 no 3 pp 81–91
59 Extensively documented in: 'Rijksbrandweeracademie te Arnhem-Schaarsbergen', Bouw 1982 no 8; offprint 'Architectuur in Bouw 1982', Rotterdam, 1983 pp 143–146
60 'Gevelconstructie nieuwbouw ministerie van Buitenlandse Zaken te 's-Gravenhage', Cement 1983 no 11 pp 711–723. Architectural documentation in Bouw 1985 no 19 pp 31–36
61 Wim J. van Heuvel: 'Een "Cité Médicale" aan de rand van de Bijlmer – het AMC tussen andere academische ziekenhuizen', architectuur/bouwen 1986 no 11 pp 37–47
62 Hans van Dijk: 'The demise of structuralism', 'Yearbook 88/89 Architecture in the Netherlands', Deventer, 1989 pp 6–10
63 Joseph Buch: 'A curious decade', 'Yearbook 89/90 Architecture in the Netherlands', Deventer, 1990 pp 6–14
64 See note 63
65 Peter Buchanan: 'Nederlandse architectuur is het spoor bijster, eigen traditie is ingeruild voor trendy internationalisme', architectuur/bouwen 1988 no 6/7 pp 63–67
66 See note 21
67 Rem Koolhaas on Dutch structuralism in International Architect 1980 no 3 pp 48–50
68 Wim J. van Heuvel: 'Het Berlijnse Kulturforum na Scharoun, Hertzberger behaalde aankoop met ontwerp Gemäldegalerie', architectuur/bouwen 1987 no 3 pp 39–48

Projects

Burgerweeshuis Amsterdam
Aldo van Eyck *Design 1955 Realization 1958–1960*

The Burgerweeshuis is at the edge of Berlage's Plan Zuid. It was built to replace the accommodation in the former monastery (now the Historical Museum) which had been in use as an orphanage in the centre of Amsterdam since the sixteenth century. The new accommodation was intended for around 125 children, varying in age from a few months to twenty years.

The building was designed as a small city. The various elements were laid out in a broad and complex pattern. A structural and constructive building system was then developed in which it was possible to realise the pattern of this society 'recognizable and homogeneous'. Within this the spaces vary from a communal inner street to the more closed individual rooms. 'While all the spaces independent of their function and span fit within the possibilities of a single architectural style, each is given its own specific meaning by its position, use, order, and further treatment; through their relation to each other, the whole and the content of the site' according to Van Eyck in a commentary in Bouwkundig Weekblad.

The complex of housing groups is spread out around a square as a transitional element from the city to the home. It begins on the street side as an open space which becomes bordered as one approaches the entrances, beneath the staff accommodation. Once inside, there is an inner street on which eight housing zones are located. The inner city street-like character of the entrance is emphasised by the use of smooth masonry, concrete and the view of surrounding building parts, patios and the surroundings. Much attention has been devoted to the details of the transitions between interior and exterior. The various housing groups are also attuned to the specific age groups in terms of layout. In order to profit as much as possible from the sun a pattern was created with many recesses and patio-like spaces at the edges.

The complex is built on a pattern of domes with a bay size of 3.6 x 3.6 metres. The round columns are alternated with wall surfaces of brick, with use being made of a 'doubly thick' brick. On the columns and masonry are architraves 50 cm high with a horizontal opening in which much glass has been placed. The floor constructions are, as is the dome roof, built in concrete. Above the communal space of each group a big dome has been placed with a surface equal to that of nine small domes.

In 1986 far-reaching renovation plans were drawn up for the complex. It was considered demolishing a part which was no longer in use. An international campaign for preservation led to the agreement to realise a new building elsewhere, which would meet new requirements with regard to child care. In a process of renovation and restoration under the supervision of Aldo and Hannie van Eyck, a part was ready for use in the spring of 1991 for the Berlage Instituut, a postgraduate architectural training institute.

Spatial succes-
sion of places
between city
and front door
as 'a score for
coming and
going'

1　sculpture
2　bus
3　service
4　child
5　seat
6　bicycles
7　director

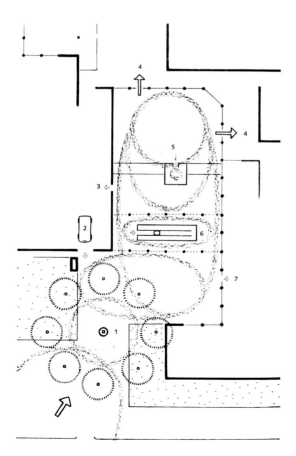

Ground floor

1 department for boys 14-18
2 department for girls 14-18
3 department for boys 10-14
4 department for girls 10-14
5 department for children 6-10
6 department for children 4-6
7 department for children 2-4
8 baby department
9 sick bay
10 party hall
11 theatre and gymnastics hall
12 director, psychologist, teamleader and staff
13 administration and archives
14 staffroom and library
15 service hall
16 garage
17 central linen-room
18 central kitchen, director's dwelling
19 teamleader's dwelling
20 entrance to bicycle shed

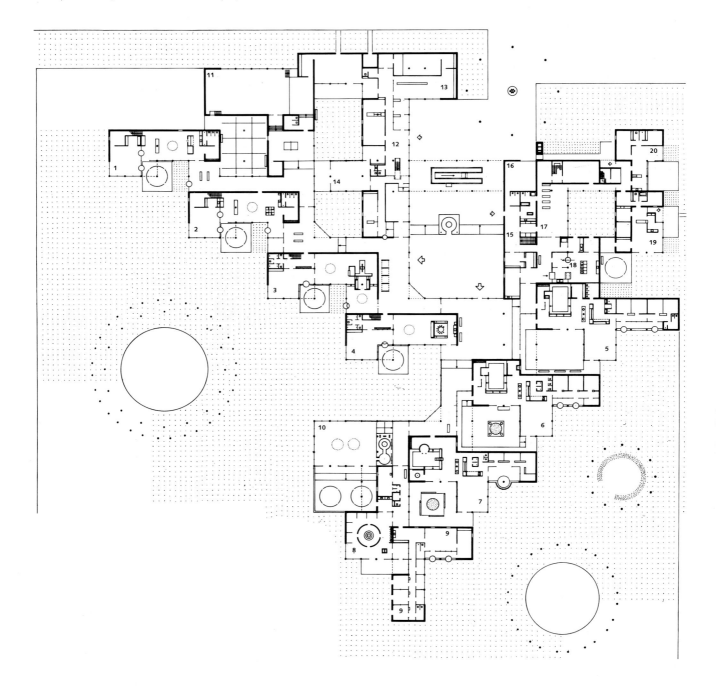

1 sleeping quarters boys 14-18   3 sleeping quarters boys 10-14   5 meeting room
2 sleeping quarters girls 14-18   4 sleeping quarters girls 10-14   6 rooms of resident staff

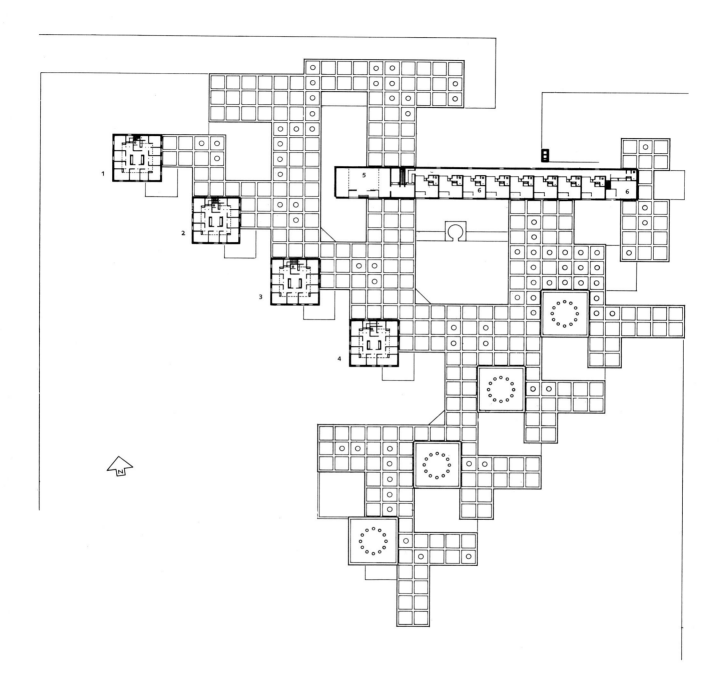

The forecourt as transitional area
between the city and the entrance

The clear structure of the skeleton, supplemented by loadbearing brickwork is visible both inside and outside

One of the restored rooms for the Berlage Instituut is being used as a communal meeting place

Prix de Rome **Study for a children's village**

Joop van Stigt *Design 1962*

For the final round of the Prix de Rome, a competition for architects under the age of 35 which is held every four years, in 1962 a design was requested for 'a village for children – a village like a house'. It involved accommodation for children in various age groups and of various nationalities. As location a site was given at the edge of the Utrecht Heuvelrug on a foreland of the Rhine.

The programme of requirements mentioned 24 'family dwellings' for sixteen children with rooms for carers, teacher and classroom. For general activities a 'village centre' was required which would include a hall for six hundred people and a series of smaller spaces for activities such as gymnastics, dancing, library, exhibitions, training and the like. Furthermore an open-air theatre, sports areas, playing field, children's farm and housing for staff were included.

In various previous study plans Joop van Stigt had developed floor plan forms of two squares partially overlapping each other diagonally: a ninth part in the 'House for Princess Beatrix', 1958, and a quarter in 'Nursing Buildings on Sloping Site', around 1961. The telescoping of the squares produced a sheltered entrance zone in the axil of both squares, an increase in sunlight-catching walls, whereby the orientation became unimportant.

For the children's village Van Stigt used this configuration of two squares as the point of departure, linked to a skeleton of columns, beams and parapets. The focus of the village was formed by the community centre, with the largest communal space. Around this hall were smaller rooms with a standard configuration and joins for rafters, as with the side aisles of Gothic churches. The immediately adjacent spaces could be used in open relation with the main space. The construction had a pyramidic construction with above the larger space on the ground level a chain of basic floor plan forms in which the top floor consisted of a single double square sandwiched together.

The jury for the Prix de Rome, including Bakema and Apon from the Forum editorial board, greatly esteemed the design and noted a great freedom in the numerical groupings within the form of the chosen structure. 'Van Stigt goes further than the usual pattern size with the goal of replacing the structural composition with this scale by a full figure, which is created from a band grid, columns, walls and parapets. In doing so he found an architectural germ cell, so that where necessary the horizontal and vertical linkage by means of the structure with the same fugal organising process becomes a single form... By centralising care and therefore not deviating from the programme, he found a great freedom for the layout of the house in terms of family and language area.'

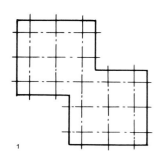

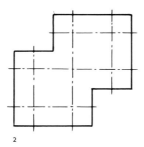

Overlapping squares as basis for the floor plan of three successive study designs

1   house for Princess Beatrix, 1958
2   nursing buildings on a sloping site, 1961
3   children's village Prix de Rome, 1962

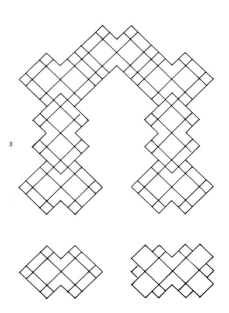

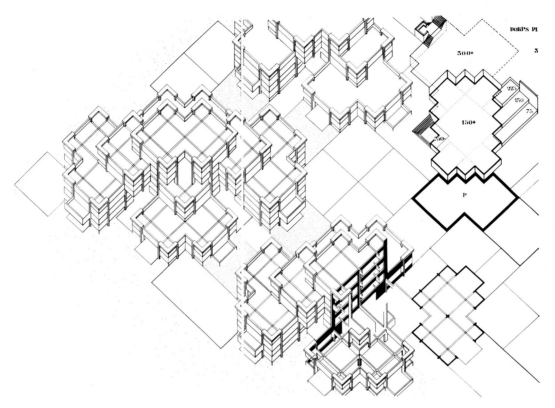

In the presentation of the design the emphasis was on the skeleton which would remain visible inside and outside as the element in the architecture giving it form

Chapel for 'Kerk en Wereld' Driebergen

Aldo van Eyck *Design 1963–1964*

Commissioned by the Protestant training institute 'Kerk en Wereld' in Driebergen, the Prof.dr. G. van der Leeuwstichting set a multiple commission for the design of a chapel on the site of the institute. The architects G. Boon, Aldo van Eyck, Herman Hertzberger, E.J. Jelles, Joop van Stigt, Jan Verhoeven, Piet Blom and Karel Sijmons were invited. The latter declined to participate. The design by Aldo van Eyck, 'The Wheels of Heaven' received first prize from the jury on which sat the architects H. Brouwer, Jaap Bakema and Gerrit Rietveld, among others.

In the sober programme of requirements a chapel or church space was requested which would be suitable for multiple use by anything from a few to three hundred people. According to his commentary Van Eyck sought a multi-central space which would not be a-central, a clearly articulated space. Between the two forecourts with entrances, four round spaces were positioned, open to a central transition area. Three of these space elements were around the lectern; the fourth space with seating in the round was envisaged for smaller gatherings, but within the same large space. Above each circle Van Eyck designed a double roof construction for daylight, which are rotated, in twos, ninety degrees around the diagonal: 'The Wheels of Heaven'. The skylights offer contact with the world outside the chapel, with a view of clouds and trees ('tree-nibblers') with birds flying around. The construction consisted of round columns of concrete with screen-like walls between them under a frame of straight and curved concrete beams as horizontal arches.

Unlike the Burgerweeshuis, here a freely interpreted measurement system has been used for the construction, in which the round columns are placed at an alternating distance from each other. Across the diagonal from the forecourts corresponding building volumes were created. The intersection of both diagonals also forms the mid-point between the three circles which leads to a complex diagonality that according to Van Eyck contributes to the required multi-centrality in multi-functional use. The design was never built.

The maquette in the exhibition of the six designs in the Stedelijk Museum in Amsterdam

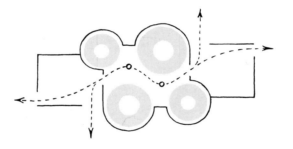

Four circles with two foci at the access between two forecourts

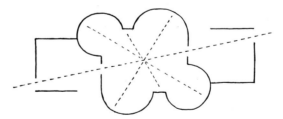

The various diagonals intersect at a central point

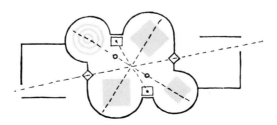

The four spaces can serve for various activities separately

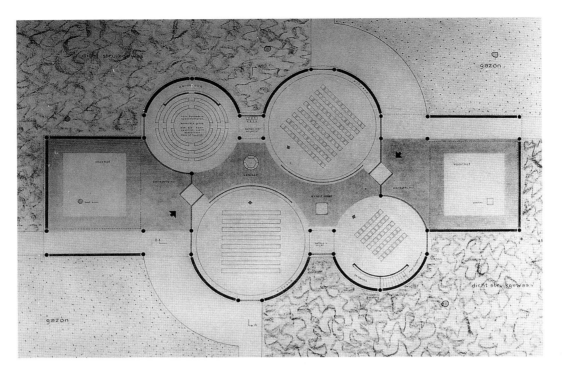

Floor plan of the church on a
wooded site alternated with lawn

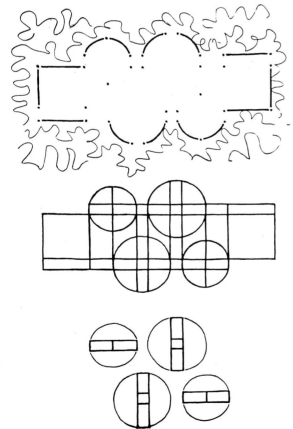

Over the round columns – with
disc-shaped walls between
them – there is a grid of beams
with skylights above them like
'The Wheels of Heaven'

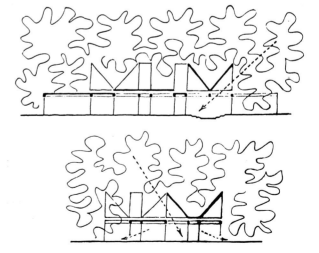

Temporary student restaurant University of Twente Enschede

Piet Blom *Design and realization 1962 – 1964*

The urban designers of the University of Twente, W. van Tijen and S.J. van Embden, nominated Piet Blom to convert an existing farmhouse with shed on the estate of Drienerlo into a temporary student restaurant. After completion of a definitive student restaurant the converted farmhouse would serve as a meeting room and campus restaurant.

One of the ideas behind the brief was the maintenance of the traditional farmhouse as a reminder of the earlier functions on the estate. As well as this the urban designers expected a 'sharp contrast which threatens to come into being between the centre, which is to be treated somewhat formally, and the nearby "rustic" farmhouse.' The wooden skeleton within the loadbearing walls was extensively changed, with the roof forms and outer walls also undergoing extensive change. The construction was visible everywhere and at some points was visible outside in partly open extensions like loggias and terraces. Newly added beams were joined to existing columns and beams with shoes of steel plates. In this way the skeleton retained a dominant character of repetitions of columns, beams and rails which together show the image of a structuring construction. Large voids and newly introduced differences in level are situated under an almost completely new roofscape of pitched roofs with ceramic tiles.

Because the masonry together with the wooden skeleton also has a loadbearing function, the conversion cannot be called a pure example of structuralism. However, the spatial transition from interior to exterior does give shape to the Forum idea.

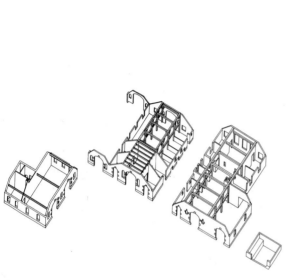

The original structure

The adjusted and extended bearing structure

The structure is visible everywhere in
the interior. Spatious voids ensure an
optimal relation between ground floor
and first floor

Staff canteen University of Twente Enschede

Joop van Stigt *Design 1963 Realization 1964*

According to the programme of requirements, the staff canteen for the University of
Twente had to be usable by both smaller groups of users and larger groups up to five
hundred people. The building site available was close to the entrance of the campus,
at the side of the main access road, and near Piet Blom's student restaurant. Both
buildings are situated in a green, wooded strip. Van Stigt sought a living-room style
atmosphere for the users who work all day in strongly-lit halls and laboratories. He
also wanted to apply the construction as both a space-forming and space-binding
element. A wooden construction was chosen, related to the natural surroundings.
The difficult building market was the reason for the choice of a prefabricated building method.

On the concrete floor a skeleton of laminated redwood was erected. The columns
support cruciform roof floors, built up from five squares with in the inner corners
small squares which link up with them. Three of these basic shapes are joined together with a fourth higher roof element placed in the centre. In publications shortly
after the building the configuration was also described as constructed of squares
which overlap to a small extent, as that was clearly the case with earlier designs by
Joop van Stigt (see his design for the Prix de Rome). In an isometeric section however, Van Stigt showed that the cruciform configuration was the basic principle, supported by eight columns halfway along the cross-wings.

The prefabricated beams are connected together by clip connections in the corners
and have been made into eaves on site. Beams of laminated redwood were also used
to form the parapets. Double-glazing was applied throughout. Because of the large
dimensions of these windows the construction of columns and narrow corner posts
has remained clearly identifiable.

Since the staff canteen was moved to Piet Blom's De Bastille, Joop van Stigt's building has housed various other university services, so that the undivided interior has
been altered into separate work spaces. Because of this the spatial character has
been lost to a great extent.

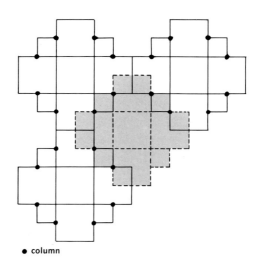

● column

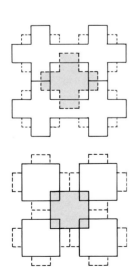

Structural construction of the linked cruciform of five squares
with smaller squares in the corners. The most central cruciform
roof surface has a higher level. On the right, the interpretations
of the basic form: cross or square

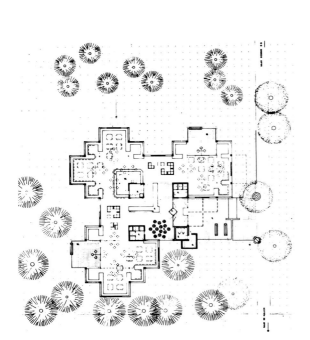

Floor plan

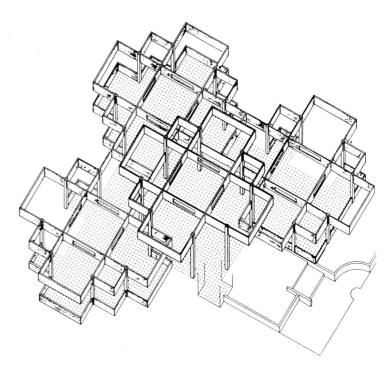

Isometry of the skeleton, built entirely of laminated wood

Sculpture pavilion for Sonsbeek Arnhem

Aldo van Eyck *Design and realization 1965–1966*

For the fifth international sculpture exhibition Sonsbeek '66 Aldo van Eyck designed a pavilion for small sculptures. The sculptures of Jean Arp, Constantin Brancusi, Max Ernst, Alberto Giacometti, Barbara Hepworth, Shinkichi Tajiri and Antoine Pevsner among others were exhibited in and around the pavilion, which was only temporary, just like the famous sculpture pavilion by Gerrit Rietveld. This had been erected in the summer of 1955 and in 1965 was rebuilt in the sculpture garden of the Rijksmuseum Kröller-Müller on the Hoge Veluwe in Otterlo.

Among the trees of the Sonsbeek park Van Eyck designed a pavilion of six parallel-positioned walls, built in rough concrete blocks, with narrow streets between them around two and a half metres wide. These structuring walls were equipped at various points with passageways and semi-circular bulges. On a pattern of squares, simple steel beams lay across the walls with narrow frames above them and a roof covering of transparent plastic. The sculptures stood on low pedestals which were made of the same concrete blocks.

Although the pavilion did not need a skeleton, the parallel-positioned walls occupy a clear structuring position within the design. Characteristic of structuralism is the free manipulation of these walls with semi-circular bulges of smaller and larger diameter. Together with the wall openings, diagonally oriented perspectives were created. Despite the simplicity of architectural means a wealth of diversified spaces was created with the sculptures placed in them.

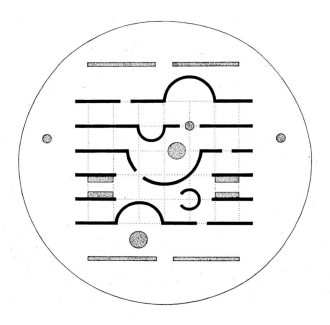

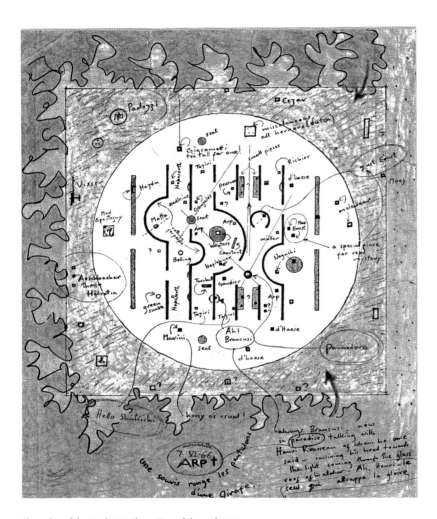

Floor plan of the pavilion with position of the sculptures

Town hall Valkenswaard
Herman Hertzberger *Design 1966*

For the building of a new town hall a multiple commission was given to the architects Dick Apon, J.L.C. Choisy, Joost van der Grinten, Herman Hertzberger and A. van Kranendonk. The architect J.C. Froger and H. Brouwer sat on the jury. The town hall was intended for a municipality with a population of 45,000 and had to be expandable for a municipal growth to 70,000 inhabitants. Because the new building was projected on the site of the old town hall, a phased building process had to be borne in mind, so that no temporary accommodation would be needed. Hertzberger designed a town hall which is constructed from 'towers' with voids between them. These towers, two and three storeys above the ground level, were linked by bridges on the axes of the square floor forms. In order to achieve a good spatial relationship between the floors, the voids were enlarged at the corners of the towers, which also led to a better division of the columns over the floor surface. This grid of square towers, 5.4 x 5.4 metres, with a two-sided band grid 4.4 metres broad, was the point of departure for the design.

In the first phase it was planned to build eleven towers, in which all special functions such as council hall and wedding hall, steps and so on were included. After demolition of the old town hall it would be expanded to sixteen towers. With further growth of the municipality the building could grow to twenty eight towers. Flexible use was simple because growing departments could make use of an adjoining floor, while surrounding departments could move up.

Notable was the manipulation of the grid. Around the main stairs the columns were included in sliding walls with the length of the stairs arm's length. At the round committee rooms the columns were included in the walls. By use of split-level floors council and marriage hall acquired a height of one and a half floors.

In his commentary Herman Hertzberger wrote: 'The town hall has to be essentially anti-monumental in the sense that monumentality is connected to power. The town hall has to be essentially monumental in the sense that monumentality is connected to democracy... Public and officials come to visit each other.' As well as this the construction in towers is a valuable adjustment in scale with regard to the existing buildings in the surroundings. The jury preferred another design, so it was not built.

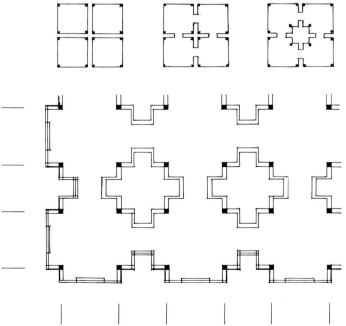

The construction of the floor plan
with square 'towers', linked by
'bridges' and enlargement of the
voids

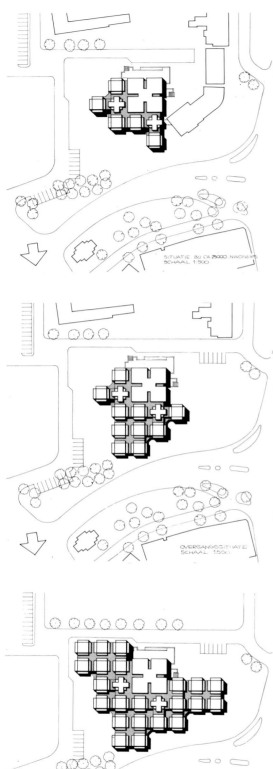

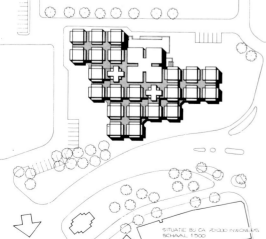

Three phases in the growth
of the municipality from
around 25,000 to 70,000
inhabitants, as that could
be expressed in the extension of the town hall

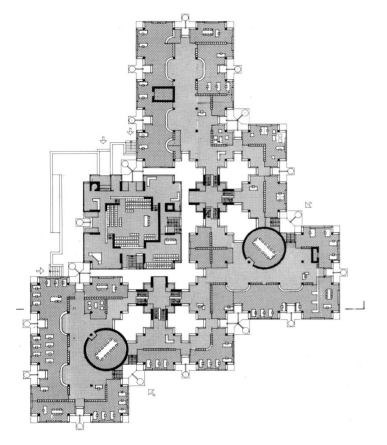

Ground floor

Cross section of the council hall

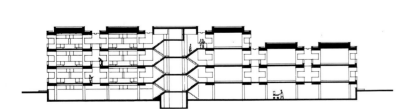

Cross section of the main stairs

Town hall Amsterdam

Herman Hertzberger, Leo Heijdenrijk, Gert Boon and Jan Verhoeven *Design 1967–1968*

In 1967 the municipality of Amsterdam set an international competition for a new town hall, after a national competition in 1936 had ultimately failed to deliver a satisfactory design. The first round consisted of an ideas competition for which 802 designs were submitted. The jury with Sir Robert H. Matthew (Great Britain), Prof. J. Schader (Switzerland), F.J. van Gool ('Dutch' architect with Belgian nationality), H.A. Maaskant and P. Zanstra (both Dutch) selected seven designs for the closed second round of the competition. This included a single structuralist design by Leo Heijdenrijk. Herman Hertzberger's design dropped out in the first round, but was widely applauded in the Dutch architectural world for the architectural quality and as an example of structuralism. The designs by Gert Boon and Jan Verhoeven also attracted attention because of their structuralist intentions, even though on a larger level of scale.

Herman Hertzberger's design has a diagonal from the Blauwbrug to the north with a public pedestrian route. At right angles to this there is another diagonal access with a second bridge over the Amstel and a linking pedestrian bridge. Around the intersection of the diagonals was the main entrance with central facilities and adjoining public spaces such as council and meeting rooms. The centre or heart of the town hall created in this fashion is surrounded by office spaces which, just as in Hertzberger's competition design for the town hall of Valkenswaard, are housed in 'towers'. Here, Hertzberger chose towers eight metres square with three metres space between them. Bridges link the towers together with cruciform voids. Columns mark the spot of the connecting bridges and at the outer walls are replaced by round columns. The solution is a simplified version of the design for Valkenswaard, but was not further developed in the first round of the ideas competition. Because of the size of specific spaces such as big halls these are encased as larger-scale building volumes in the structure of the surrounding office spaces. As well as a strong connection with the existing urban fabric the design also seeks a rapprochement with the width of the individual canal facades in the Amsterdam centre through the rhythm of towers eight metres broad.

The complex was situated quite close to the Amstel with the northwestern facade directly on the water of the broadened Zwanenburgwal, to knit the building to the water of the city.

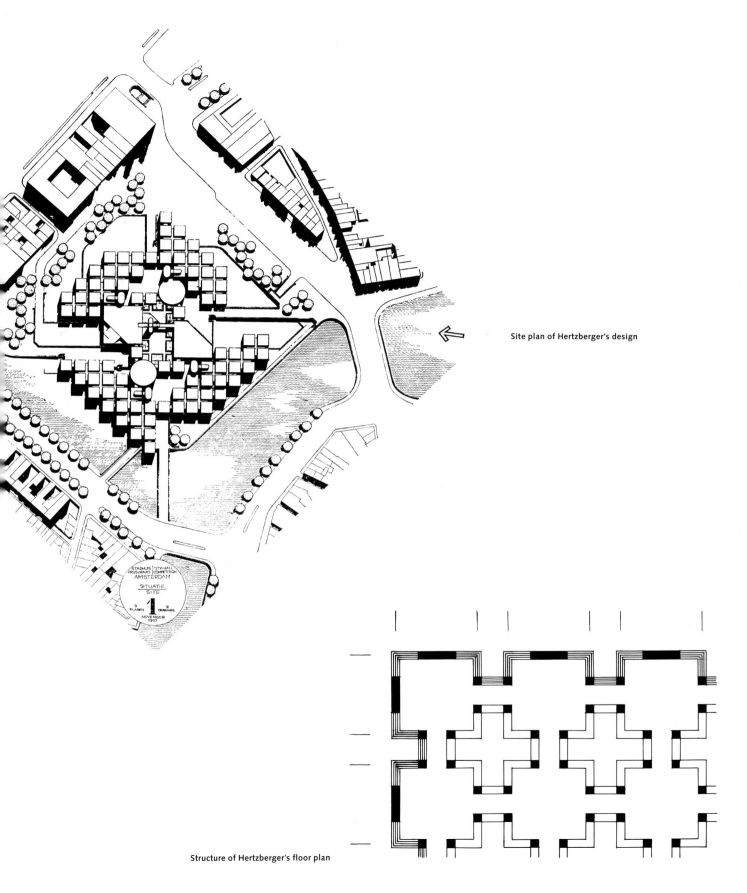

Site plan of Hertzberger's design

Structure of Hertzberger's floor plan

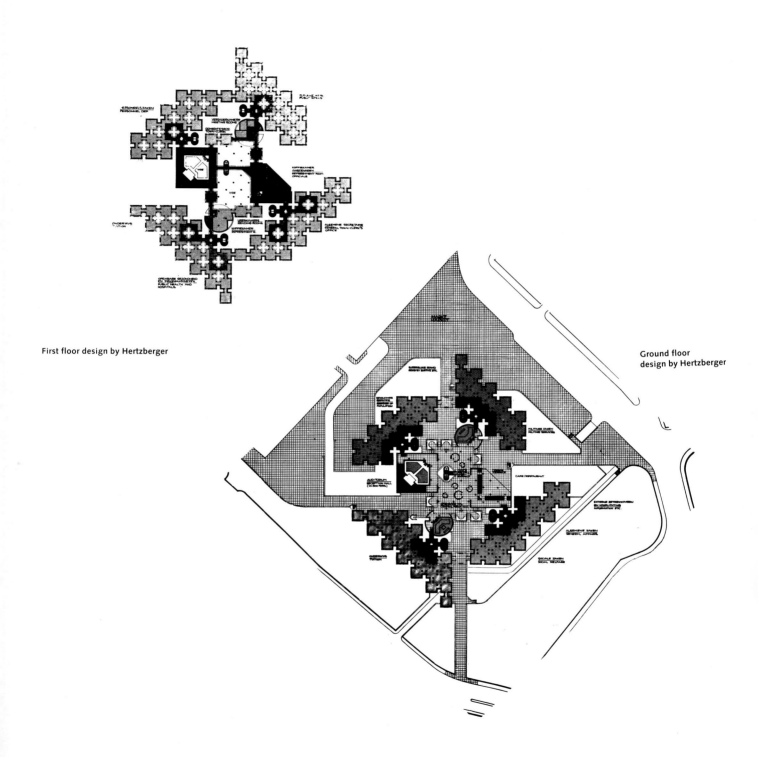

First floor design by Hertzberger

Ground floor
design by Hertzberger

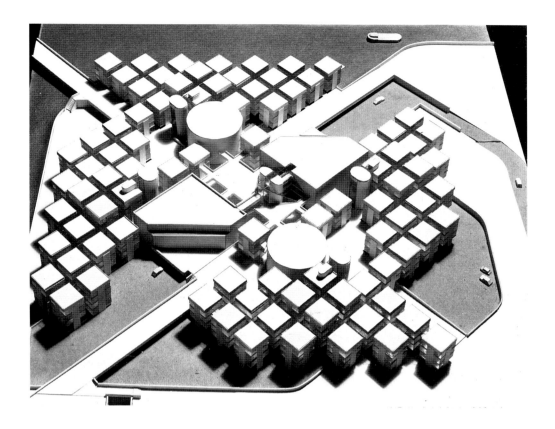

Maquette of Hertzberger's design

Herman Hertzberger, **Leo Heijdenrijk**, Gert Boon and Jan Verhoeven

The structuralist character of the competition design by Leo Heijdenrijk arose mainly in the development in the second closed round. In his design too the diagonal from the Blauwbrug played an important role, but as a boundary between the land and the meeting between Amstel and Zwanenburgwal, widened at the corners.
On the street level Heijdenrijk situated the Waterlooplein market under the building, bordering the widened water with jetties which were also partly envisaged as islands in the water under the building. The main floor of the town hall, 3.6 metres above street level, was accessible for cars and cyclists along ramps.
Towers measuring 14.5 x 14.5 metres were envisaged around a central space with a space between them of 1.5 metres. The floor construction of the towers consisted of a grid of beams which dropped in height towards the edges; the support consisted of four columns placed in the centre. Along the edges of each floor surface a small square void was designed in the middle; two short bridges linked the towers at the sides. The building height varied from three to seven storeys, and along the edges linked up with the existing buildings across from it. The strong connection with the urban fabric was emphasised in the design by the market under the town hall, the way the building is interwoven with the water and the landing facilities along the jetties. Due to the considerably larger size of the towers, articulation of the outer walls is less emphatically attuned to the lot size of the Amsterdam canal facades as in Hertzberger's design.

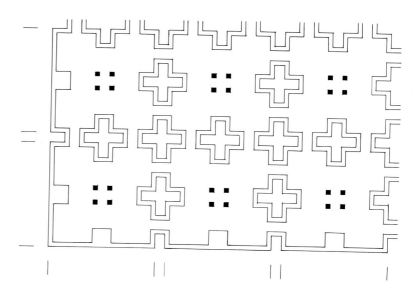

Structural floor plans of Heijdenrijk

Maquette of design by Heijdenrijk

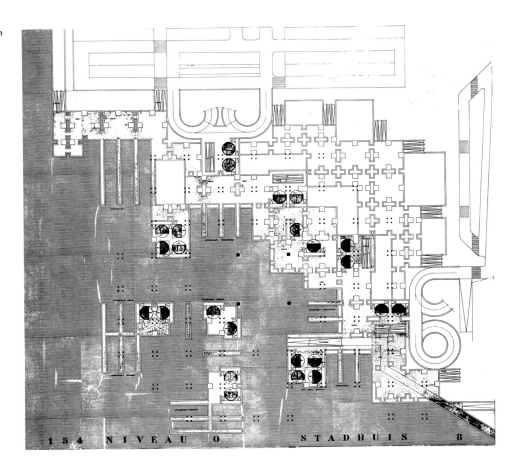

Ground floor of Heijdenrijk design

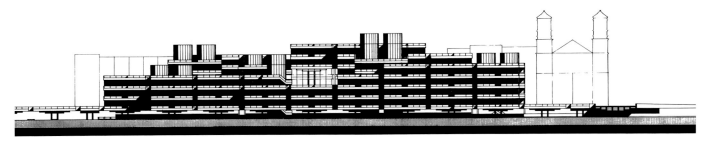

Southwest elevation of Heijdenrijk design

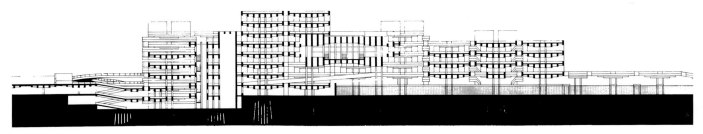

Cross section of Heijdenrijk design

First floor of Heijdenrijk design

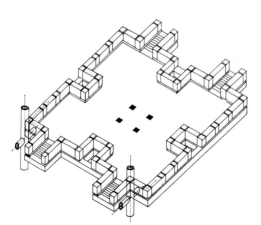

Plan of Heijdenrijk's balustrades

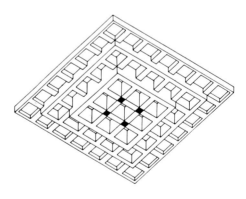

View from below of Heijdenrijk's grid of beams

Herman Hertzberger, Leo Heijdenrijk, **Gert Boon** and Jan Verhoeven

Architect Gert Boon, who like Hertzberger had been an editor of Forum, developed a structuralist design on a considerable larger scale. The building was designed on a grid of squares measuring 22.5 x 22.5 metres, with a space between them of 4.5 metres. The squares are impinged on by exterior spaces with a basic form of a quarter circle which in the design led to semi-circular round exterior spaces alongside each other. At some points extensions have been included in the rounded exterior spaces on the ground floor which utilise the entire square, with above them terrace-shaped receding extensions which become smaller as they go higher.

The loadbearing structure consists of cores of concrete of five by five metres in which stairs, toilet facilities, lifts, wiring and service spaces were envisaged, with round columns at the connections of the elements.

The building height varied from two to five floors. The water of the Amstel and Zwanenburgwal was broadened at some points to the outer walls in order to link up with the building volume. On the ground floor the structure around the big entrance hall was left partly open between cores and sliding walls.

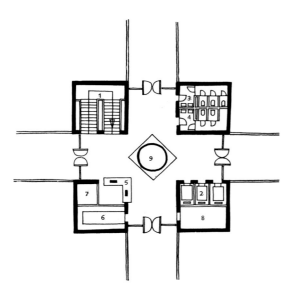

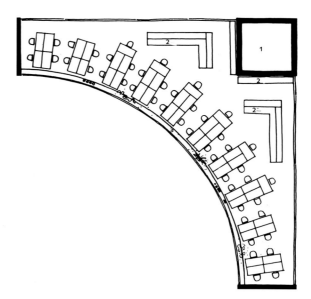

Vertical core of Boon design

		5	messenger
		6	cloakroom
1	stairwell	7	storage
2	lifts	8	service
3,4	toilets	9	void with tabletop

Boon design for office space

1 vertical core
2 cupboards
3 window-sill

Maquette of Boon design

Second floor

1 meeting room of Mayor
  and aldermen
2 municipal secretary
3 void
4 gallery of council hall
5 balcony of hall
6 music gallery
7 reading rooms
8 meeting room Mayor
  and aldermen
9 coffee room

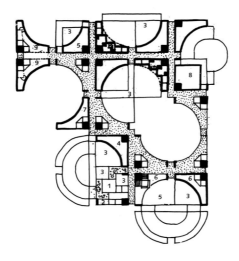

First floor

1 Mayor
2 council hall
3 large receptions
4 terraces
5 large hall with gallery
6 hall gallery
7 conference room
8 cafe-restaurant
9 coffee room
10 voids
11 office space
12 first class marriage

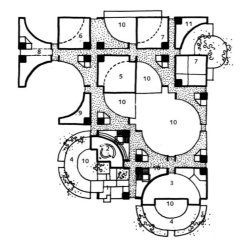

Ground floor of Boon design

1 central hall
2 marriage
3 banns
4 metro hall
5 porter, press, police
6 coffee bar
7 entrance to restaurant
8 entrance to car park
9 registry office
10 covered quay
11 marina quay
12 town hall square

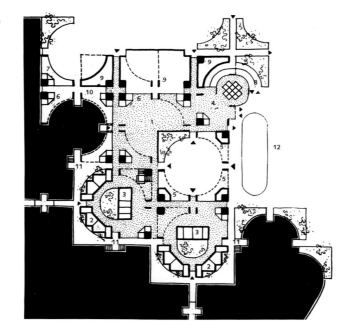

Herman Hertzberger, Leo Heijdenrijk, Gert Boon and **Jan Verhoeven**

The design by architect Jan Verhoeven was more general in structure. Cruciform floors were supported by vertical cores consisting of two round columns with space between them for vertical transport and wiring. The cores were linked together by cylindrical beams under the floors. At some points the outer row of columns was in the water.

Within the structure it was attempted to have spatial construction with trapezium-shaped cross sections of the various parts, consisting of a broad floor strip with straight parapets and above them sloping glass walls which ended against the box girder. The structure had a very open character because at various points there was a lot of space left open between the carriers of cores and cruciform floors.

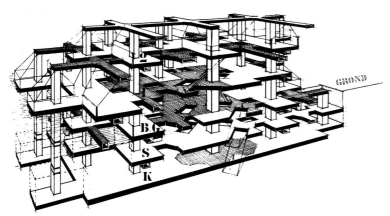

Isometric section of Verhoeven design

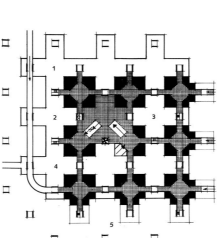

Ground floor of Verhoeven design

1 registry office
2 restaurant
3 coffee room
4 marriage rooms
5 boat moorings

Second floor

1 aldermen
2 meeting room
3 party rooms
4 reception room
5 council hall
6 reception room

The Zilveren Schor Arnemuiden
Onno Greiner *Design 1962–1964 Realization 1964–1967*

The Zilveren Schor is a meeting centre for Dutch youth where groups and individual visitors often lodge for periods of some days to a week. Queen Juliana and Prince Bernhard donated the complex to youth on the occasion of their silver wedding anniversary. It is located on crown property, a triangular piece of salt marsh outside the dikes which became dry when the Veerse Meer was enclosed.

The centre was designed completely on the ground floor, because of ease of access for physically handicapped visitors. The pyramidic roofs offer room for expansion at various points.

The various functions such as gathering together, eating, liturgical space and sleeping are housed in pavilions under a pyramid, linked by a system of corridors with a flat roof. This creates a small urban settlement surrounded by a forest for wood production.

For the construction of the larger communal spaces a prefabricated roof construction on separate columns was used. The inner streets are also built completely in wood with big glass walls which apart from a view of the surroundings also offer the possibility of orientation within the complex. Around the wooden constructions of the pavilions, brick walls have been built, alternated with glass walls. Only for smaller rooms has the brickwork been treated as loadbearing for the roof construction. The roofs are covered with ceramic tiles.

Future extensions were taken into account in the design, and it is possible to expand the system of corridors to new pavilions.

Plan

1 main building
2 playground
3 campfire
4 sports field
5 camping site
6 marina

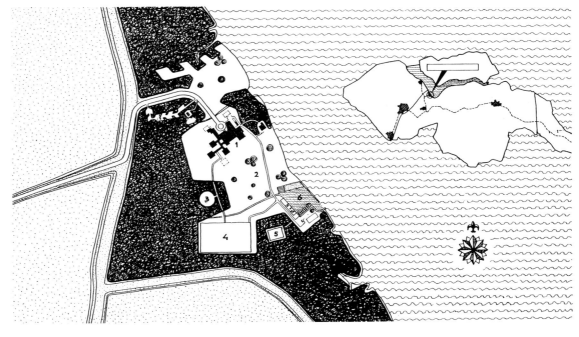

Floor plan

1   hall

2   liturgical space
3   leaders
4   service rooms/kitchen

5   eating and meeting hall
6   staff residences
7   sleeping pavilion

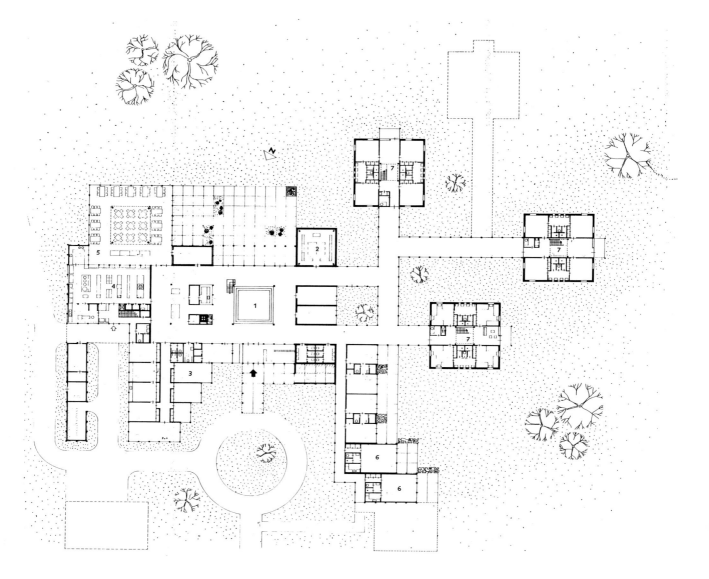

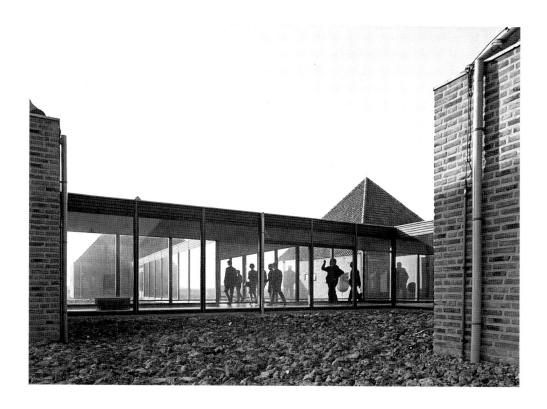

Temporary town hall Limmen

Joop van Stigt *Design and realization 1967–1968*

The rural municipality of Limmen, to the south of Alkmaar, commissioned Joop van Stigt to design a temporary town hall with a very modest budget. The building was located on the edge of the bulb fields in a flat landscape and also housed a small post office.

After his staff canteen in Drienerlo, Van Stigt once again based his design on mutual linkage of a cruciform basic configuration. The programme of requirements was limited, so that all functions could simply be housed on the ground floor. Three cruciform building sections were linked together at their ends and contain work rooms and council hall around an entrance zone in the centre building section. For toilets, kitchen and archives supplementary closed blocks, a little higher, were added in the axils of the cruciform configuration, and a glass strip between both roof levels.

Here too Van Stigt chose a wooden construction whose details, because of the temporary nature of the building, are as simple and cheap as possible. Foundations and parapets consist of prefabricated wall elements of concrete such as those which could be bought for station platforms. A wooden wall plate spreads the strain of the construction over this foundation. The roof construction consists of a stressed skin construction with beams and roof plates which are built up from two layers of plywood on a light wooden frame. In the heart of the cruciform diagonally crossing beams provide support for the roof plates; they also form a join for dividing walls if they are needed in the floor plan layout. As the walls between the columns, parapets and roof joists are completely glazed, a very transparent building was created. The temporary town hall is still in use.

Floor plan

1 hall with counters
2 secretary
3 secretary
4 Mayor
5 municipal works
6 council and marriage hall
7 post office

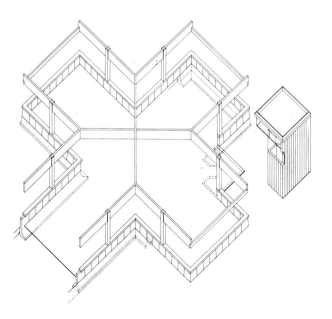

Structural layout with extra closed elements
for toilet and kitchen

Design for Church-building ideas competition Utrecht-Overvecht
Leo Heijdenrijk *Design 1968*

In 1968, the Tijdschrift voor Architectuur en Beeldende Kunst (TABK) and the Inter-diocesan committee for church-building organised an ideas competition to reconsider the place and form of church-building. Participants were free to choose a site in the Utrecht neighbourhood of Overvecht and if desired, could adapt the surroundings to the church.

Sitting on the jury were Geert Bekaert and the architects J.A. van den Berg, Sier van Rhijn, Karel Sijmons and Rein H. Fledderus as substitute member.

The design by Leo Heijdenrijk which won the first prize produced a further development of structuralism to the town planning level. In the design a grid was marked out with squares of 6.75 metres, on an open space in the neighbourhood. Within this grid bands were marked off which were used at the first floor level to include access routes for pedestrians in two directions. The construction, consisting of four columns at the corners of a square, was staggered in the grid, so that on the raised footpaths diverse spaces could be projected for the community in temporary or more definitive forms, to be later expanded or reduced. A filling in of the space between the main construction of one to two floors with usable roof terraces was borne in mind. The required church space with additional rooms was envisaged in the centre of the facilities. Although the given location was an existing residential neighbourhood with CIAM-type rows of buildings, the basic idea would be more suited to a design in a housing environment in which the design could be integrated into the town planning layout.

Within the context of an ideas competition the jury found this general 'discussion plan' a good contribution to the integration of the church into the world. The unrealized concept appeared to indicate new ways toward a structuralist-based town planning, in which the low 'church content' was embedded in other communal facilities.

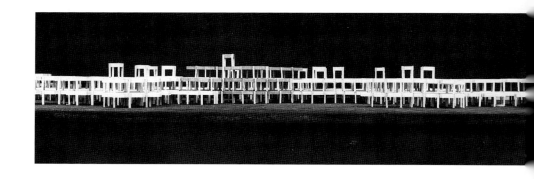

Layout of the construction

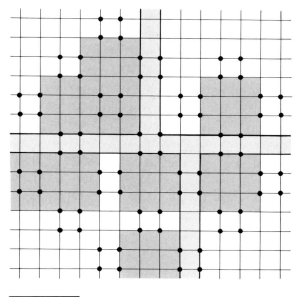

access routes

construction

filling in

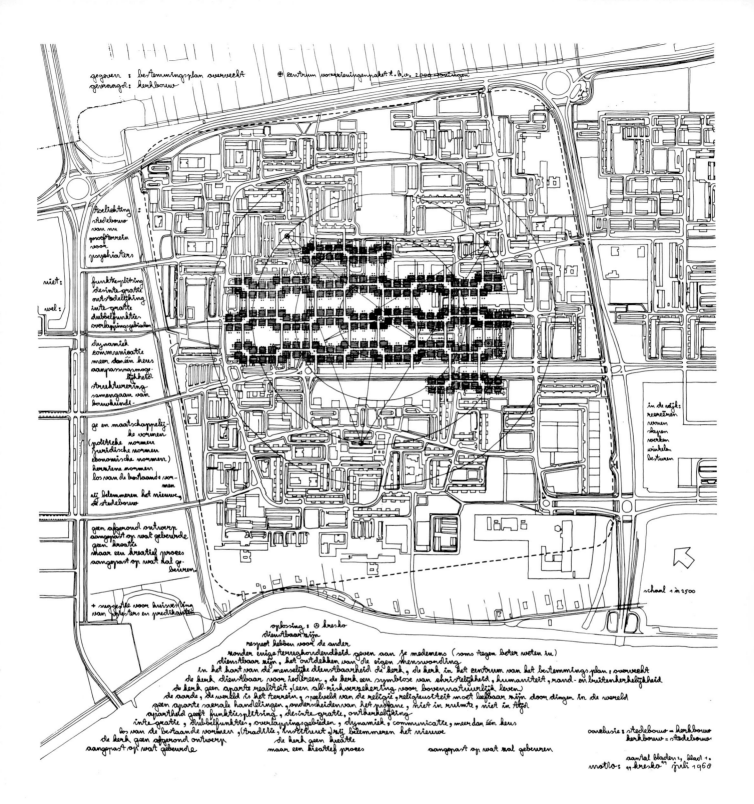

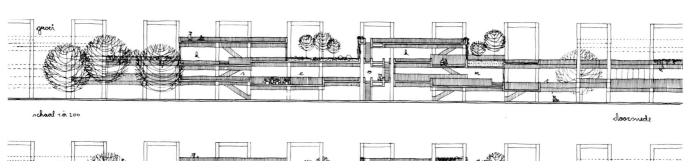

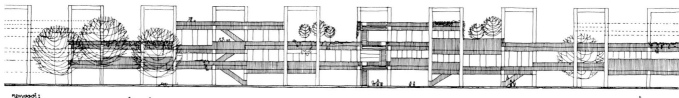

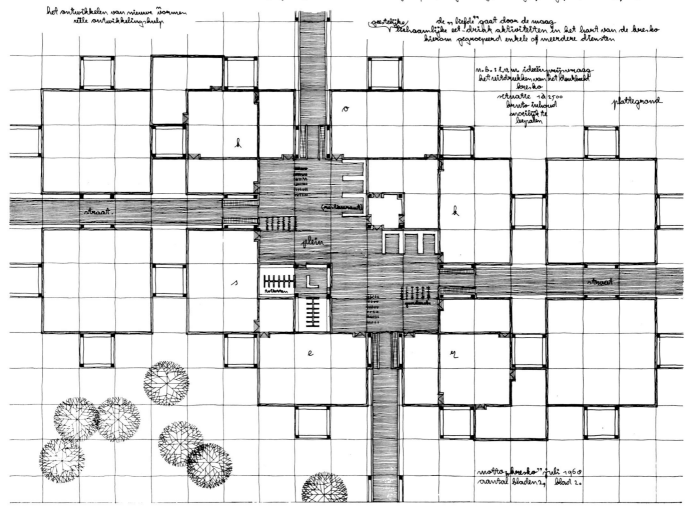

De Bastille University of Twente Enschede
Piet Blom *Design 1964–1967 Realization 1967–1969*

In accepting the brief for a definitive student restaurant for the University of Twente, Piet Blom made it a condition that he be involved in the town planning design of the centre of the campus. The original master plan by W. van Tijen and S.J. van Embden was based on a separation of functions. A broad access road divided the faculty buildings from the residential area for students. In the centre various detached buildings for various communal facilities were planned.

Piet Blom, working together with Bert Smulders, developed a strongly deviating vision. The notable access boulevard was split and built over with a complex structure in which diverse functions had to be housed. Linked to a sports field a second group of buildings was needed, which would create an 'agora', also bordered by the high-rise of the faculty building for electrical engineering and physics by Van Embden.

For both new buildings Blom and Smulders developed a basic structure which could easily be extended in any future growth of the university. The buildings could be built in different phases. The ground floor was therefore left open to a great extent, between the combined columns of the loadbearing structure, as a covered square with entrances for the upper floors, with bar, snack bar, restaurant and terraces. An elevated pedestrian route, above and along the stands of the sports ground, would link the two building structures.

The layout of this town planning study quickly turned out to be too ambitious, while the university board raised objections to a number of details such as the open ground floor. In a further brief only the restaurant was elaborated, with a future extension as second phase being taken into account. For design and development Blom founded the Werkplaats voor Publieke Werken, in which he worked together with Rob Blom of Assendelft, Lucien Lafour and Wim Samusamu.

For the restaurant, later called De Bastille, use was made of a partly prefabricated concrete construction. Rectangular floor areas of 11.43 x 6.15 metres at right angles to each other are linked in this, so that between each four elements a vertical shaft was created for wiring, lifts and the like. It made a design possible with a great number of floor levels which link up carefully with the planned activities. In the roof elongated skylights are included which allow light deep into the building volume of the complex via voids.

The construction is less clearly to be seen in the exterior because of a brick facade all around. Inside, the construction remained in view everywhere, supplemented by the vertical cores built in clean brickwork.

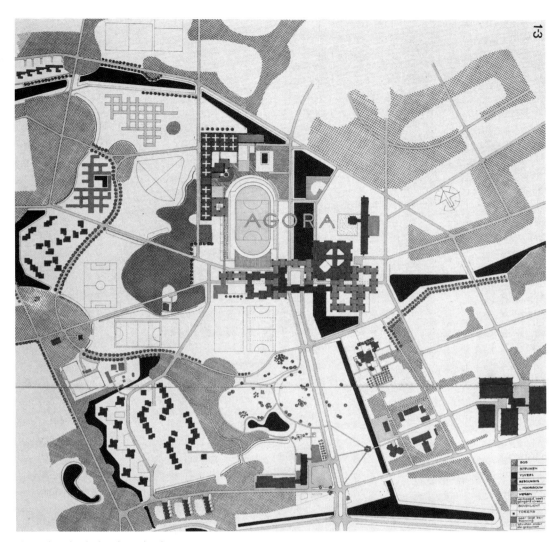

The partly realised urban design by Blom

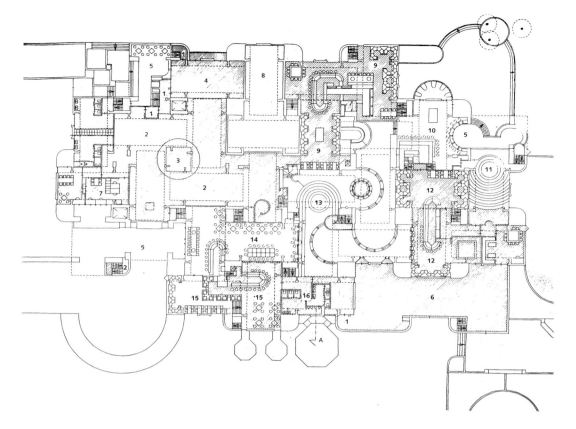

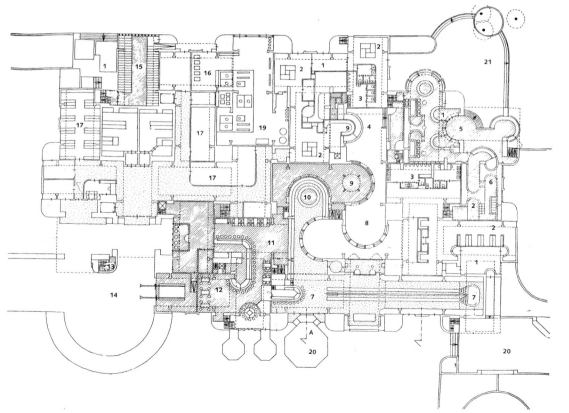

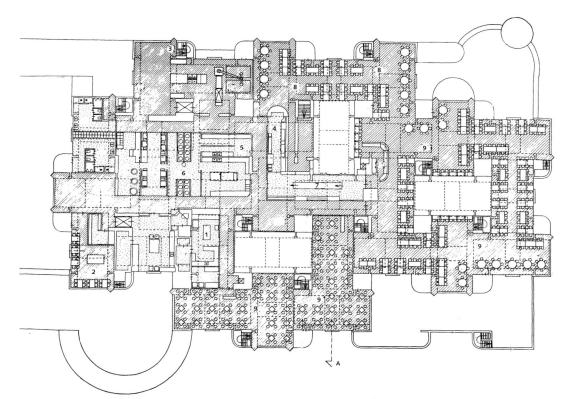

Restaurant floor

1 cold kitchen
2 staff canteen
3 to the roof terrace
4 snack bar
5 scullery
6 cooking area
7 dishwashing area
8 self-service
9 restaurant

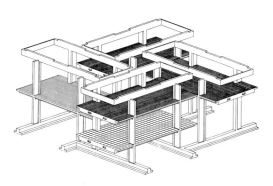

The structural construction

Cross section A

Diagoon dwellings Delft-Buitenhof
Herman Hertzberger *Design 1967–1969 Realization 1969–1971*

Commissioned by the Experimental Housing Foundation, Hertzberger designed a staggered row of eight dwellings as prototypes in which the future inhabitants could determine the floor plan themselves. The concept was based on an unbuilt suburb in the municipality of Vaassen from 1967. As well as simple alterations of the interior, various forms of extension were provided for in the design, also in the inhabited stage.

The dwellings, seven metres broad, were built in concrete blocks with floors of reinforced concrete. Fixed elements in the floor plan were the stairs and, above each other, the kitchen and bathroom. Between these fixed elements a void was fitted through the entire height of the dwelling, under a skylight with a door to the roof terrace. The various floor levels run the whole longitudinal axis of the dwelling, located split-level-style around the open space. The dwellings were delivered as shells without any interior walls. The buyers did have a design drawing however, with suggestions for further layouts with the help of interior walls and cupboards, sleeping units and additional washing facilities. The wooden walls from floor to ceiling were given a layout in which elements like fixed glass, revolving or sliding windows and closed panels could be altered or interchanged as required.

Because of the split-level layout, with growth of the number of inhabitants or a larger spatial requirement the dwelling can be simply extended by a half-floor on the roof terrace. On the ground floor the built-in garage can be converted into a hobby room or workroom by replacing the garage door with a window. The portico for the front door can be used as a spacious entrance hall by adding a glass wall in the facade. They are possibilities which were relatively easy to exploit.

Although it lacked the skeleton which is often characteristic of structuralism, the constructive structure in clean masonry of concrete blocks also remained visible in the dwelling. Characteristic of structuralism are the inbuilt flexibility and the extendability to which the inhabitants were challenged almost provocatively by the architect. In the twenty years that the dwellings have been in use, diverse use has been made of these possibilities. One of the inhabitants, the architect Carel Weeber, had large painted surfaces applied to the facade of his dwelling. Other inhabitants put a conservatory on the roof and there were also individual adjustments. Within the dwelling it is above all the open central space which invites visual and/or acoustic contact.

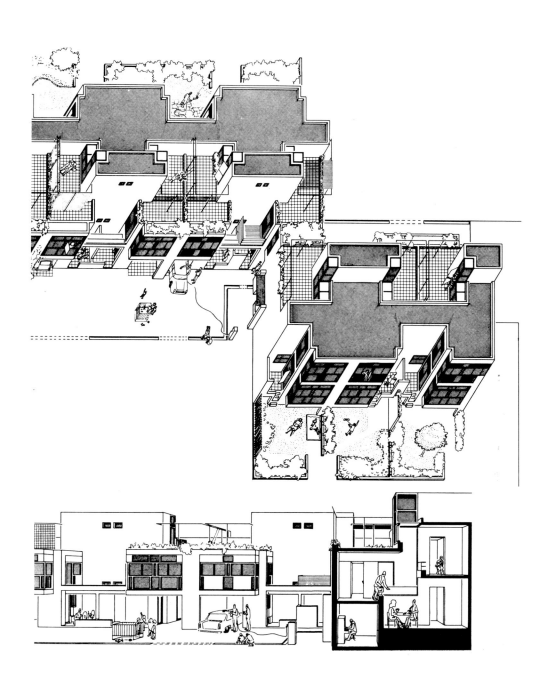

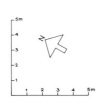

Floor plans and cross section

1   garage
2   kitchen
3   balcony
4   terrace
5   bathroom
6   tower room

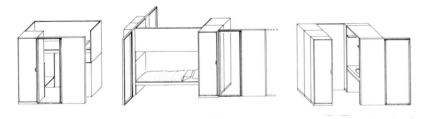

Three possibilities which include partition walls, a cell for sleeping/working, a sleeping block, and a washroom

Head offices Centraal Beheer Apeldoorn

Herman Hertzberger *Design 1967–1970 Realization 1970–1972*

The commission for the head offices of the insurance company Centraal Beheer was for 'a work area for 1000 people'. Here, Hertzberger was given the opportunity to give concrete shape to his design ideas from the competition entries for the town halls of Valkenswaard and Amsterdam. With the location at the side of the railway track it was assumed that the station would be moved, creating an entrance zone to the inner city between Hertzberger's Centraal Beheer and the office block by Wim Davidse (Kaman bureau) being built at the same time. Ultimately however, the station remained at its original location and the entrance zone was never realised. The design for Centraal Beheer was once again approached by Hertzberger through a grid, this time consisting of 'towers' measuring nine by nine metres with three metre wide voids between them under skylights and bridges for connections. With its flexible layout, the direct contacts and the anti-hierarchical organization, this solution refers to the 'office landscape' then in fashion. Each tower floor contained four work areas for one to four people with an open traffic route between them which links up with the bridges. This makes visual contact with the other floors possible for the users and it is almost impossible to 'fill in' the office landscape. Besides this, the clearly present construction with heavy columns ensures a sub-division into groups which modifies the massification of the office landscape.

The grid with towers is diagonally situated with regard to the railway line and the road. The building is sub-divided into four departments around a central hall with high intermediary spaces in the form of a sail arm. Three quadrants contain office spaces. In the lower fourth quadrant the staff restaurant is housed on the open space between the office buildings by Hertzberger and Davidse. Parking was partly located under the building. For an efficient completion groups of four columns from the upper buildings are formed into a single heavy mushroom-shaped column. These columns, poured during the work, are on a grid of around eighteen and a half metres, which is rotated thirty five degrees with regard to the office towers, and are therefore equidistant from the railway line and road.

The construction of the floors above the car park is built up from a prefabricated concrete construction of columns, main beams and floor slabs with a pressure layer. The outer and inner walls are built in clean masonry of concrete blocks, supplemented at some points by inner walls of glass bricks.

For the layout Hertzberger designed a series of desks with various possibilities for drawers, wires, uprights and facilities for telephone and individual lighting. The concrete and clean masonry which had not been finished stimulated the staff to decorate their working environment according to their own tastes with plants, posters and the like.

Maquette with new station location. The main entrance was connected to an area of shops between the two office buildings

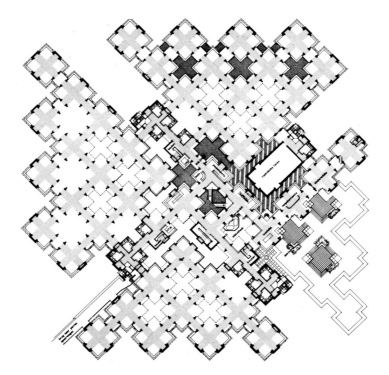

Floor plan floor 2

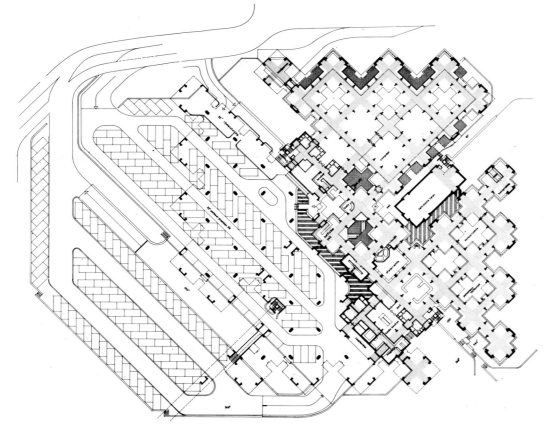

Floor plan floor 1

The pyramidically constructed complex contains parking space at the edges, partially under the building

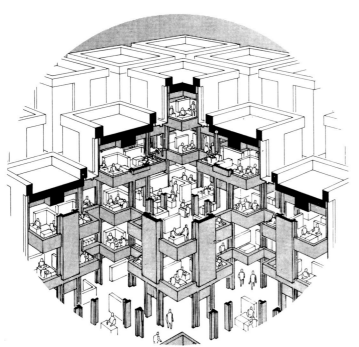

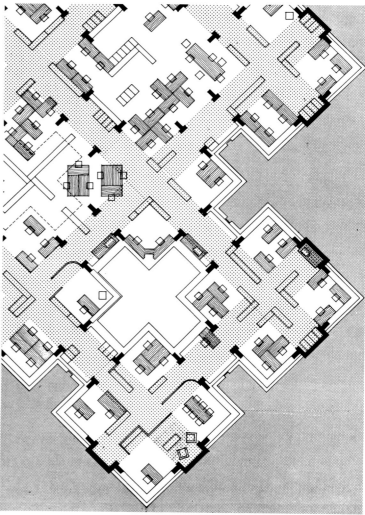

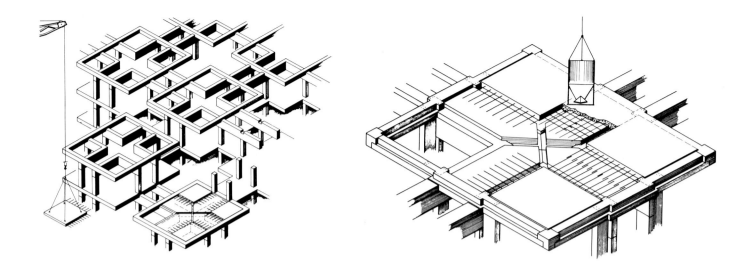

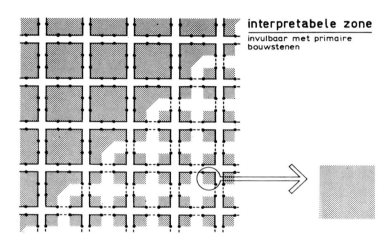

interpretabele zone
invulbaar met primaire bouwstenen

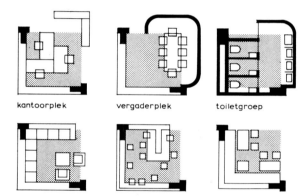

primaire bouwstenen

kantoorplek   vergaderplek   toiletgroep

The interpretable zone as this can be filled in with the building blocks on the right, including office area, meeting area, toilets, sitting room/waiting room, rest area or restaurant corner

Voids between the 'office towers' promote contact between the adjoining work stations

Public spaces in the centre of the building

Staff canteen

Parking between the mushroom columns

From urban roof to Kasbah Hengelo

Piet Blom *Study around 1966 Design 1969–1971 Realization 1972–1973*

Because of his design for the Prix de Rome and the temporary student restaurant for the University of Twente, Piet Blom was asked by A. Sjoer, technical advisor of Nedaco, to make a study for housing with a high density under roofs with ceramic tiles. This led to the concept plan 'Housing as urban roof'. In this the ground floor was used for access, parking space, storage, public greenery, a community centre, shops, restaurants and bars. Tightly packed single-family-dwellings stood on columns, provided with individual terraces of twenty to forty square metres per dwelling. The dwellings were reached by a network of pedestrian paths on the first floor with between and above them the various floors of the dwellings. As well as voids at some points in the housing roof, occasional blocks of dwellings were also left out in order to create small neighbourhood parks. Where desired the urban roof can also be made higher in order to build more urban activities under it. Blom expected a building density of one hundred dwellings per hectare where the 'the fire brigade sleeps above its red monsters, the sexton above his church, the wizard meets the architect, the tile manufacturer, the rabbi, the bath attendant, the grocer...' The socially variegated population would be given the opportunity to alter and extend their dwellings if needed, comparable to the process of growth in old city centres. The municipality of Hengelo commissioned Blom in 1969 to further develop his study, originally for a site in the inner city. At a later stage the design ended up in the postwar suburb of Groot Driene as the Kasbah. Because the design had to be built within the budget of subsidised social housing, the access with elevated pedestrian paths was dropped and many economies were needed, despite extra subsidy in the context of the 'Experimental Housing' decree by the Ministry of Public Housing and Planning.

The building density is 46 dwellings per hectare with a parking norm of 1.5 cars per dwelling. The neighbourhood includes 184 Housing Act Dwellings, a community centre, a supermarket and a number of smaller shops. A park of one fifth of a hectare is included.

The dwellings can be reached directly from the ground floor with exterior stairways. They consist of four to six rooms on one or two floors, which are openly connected to each other. Because of the high level of standardization the plan could have been built in a more industrial manner, but in Hengelo the scale was too small for that. The lower building is built in concrete at some points; the upper part of the buildings is built in red brick for the outer walls, the roofs are wood with ceramic tiles. A few years after completion research has showed that the compact style of building produced a great shortage of privacy. Also, because of the location in a suburb the open space on the ground floor was not sufficiently developed.

The Kasbah shortly before completion

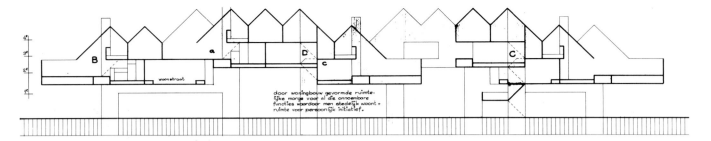

Schematic section of the urban site

Part of the floor plan with dwellings on elevated pedestrian streets

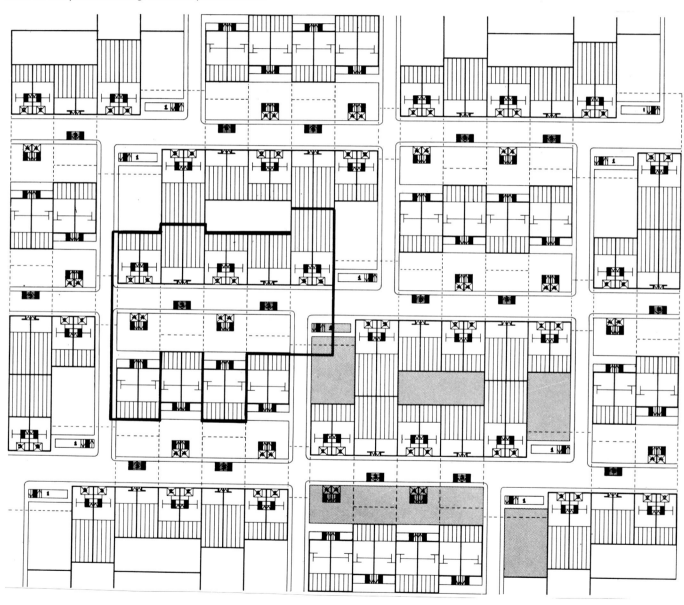

Maquette of the urban roof

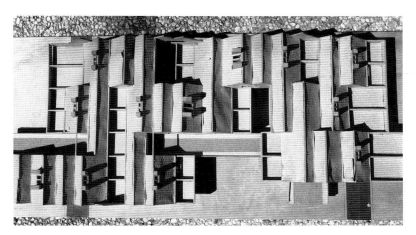

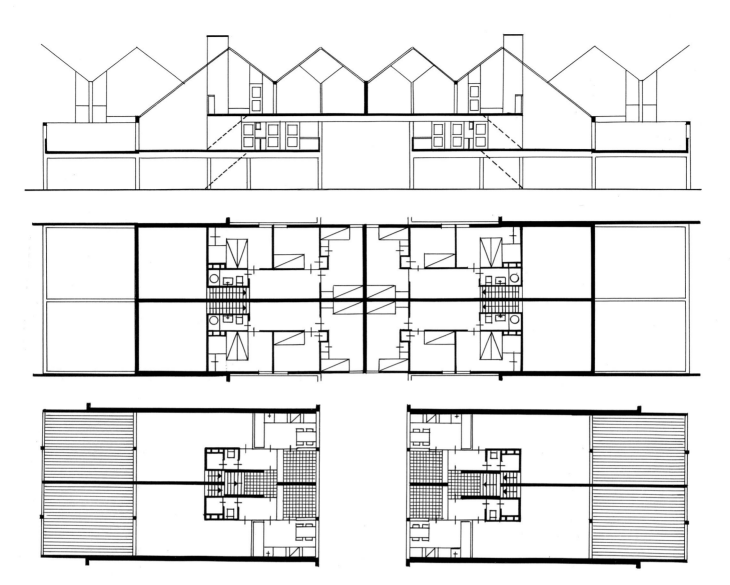

Four dwellings with four rooms on living and sleeping floor

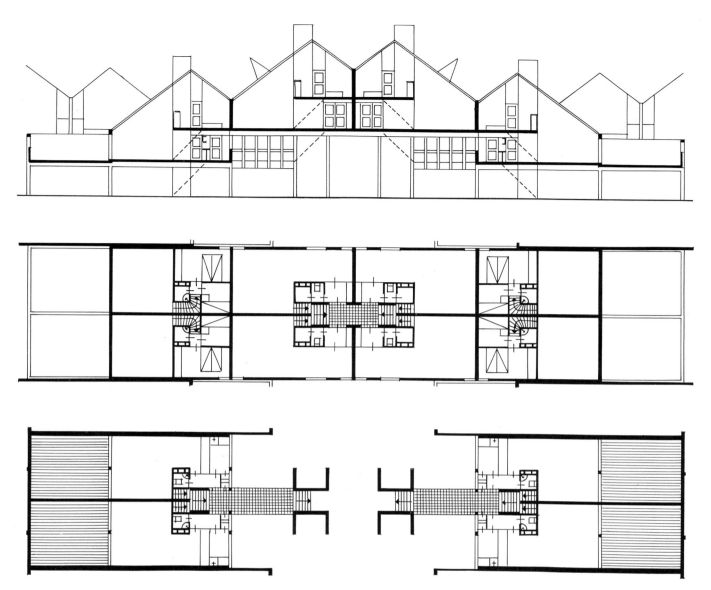

Four dwellings with three rooms and four studio dwellings between them

Multi-functional community centre 't Karregat Eindhoven

Frank van Klingeren *Design and realization 1970 – 1973*

Architect Frank van Klingeren became known in the 1970s for three community
centres. After De Meerpaal in Dronten came 't Karregat in Eindhoven and the Agora
in Lelystad. Van Klingeren often spoke to the media about the 'de-lumping' of society in order to promote an intensive mutual communication. In De Meerpaal, for
example, there was a large space for diverse manifestations and a market openly
connected to a theatre and a bar-restaurant.

In Eindhoven a gamut of activities were housed under a single roof: four schools
with 27 groups or 'classes', meeting and community rooms, a supermarket, six local
shops, a bar-restaurant, a community centre, the local library and the necessary
technical and service spaces. The public functions were around a court.

The realised design is located at the edge of a green lung in a new suburb. The construction is based on a two-sided grid of 7.2 metres. The columns of combined steel
frames are in the centre of a bay and are almost twice as high as the actual space.
Pyramidic glass roofs have been placed around the tops of the columns on the basis
of an entire bay. In both directions, these 'parasols' alternate with bays with flat
roofs. The parasols are linked by light latticework girders of steel and on this a roof
surface with a layer of wooden joists. The walls are mainly of glass with parapets and
closed sections at some points.

In the floor plan bays are set back or forward at some points and entrance zones are
pushed back under the roof in order to make the spatial transition from exterior to
interior more gradual. The architecture seems to be a precursor of the so-called
high-tech architecture, in which the construction is demonstratively displayed.

In the humane society advocated by Van Klingeren there were as few thresholds as
possible. The various parts of the building were in open contact under the continuous roof. In the schools too, an optimal openness was aimed at with classrooms
being only partly separated from each other by open cupboard walls half the height
of the room.

Very soon after use started, acoustic facilities turned out to be necessary and a start
was made with compartmentalising the complex. Until 1990 therefore, alterations
have been carried out with a certain regularity with separation of functions becoming more a reality. Although the 'de-lumping' has therefore been set back to a great
extent, the structure with the parasol-shaped column tops remain a structuring element in many spaces.

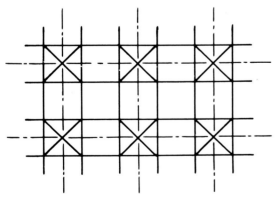

Layout of the structural grid

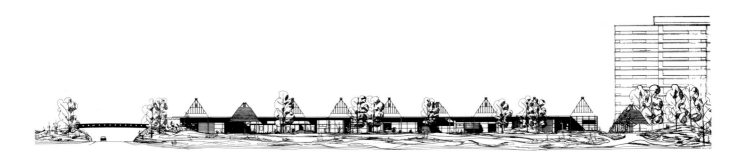

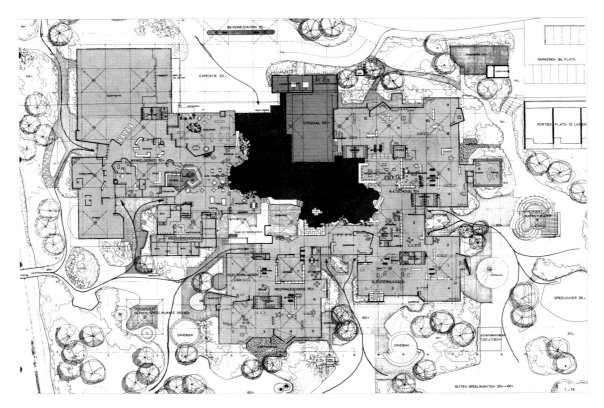

Floor plan and elevation

Exterior with free-standing frame on the schoolyard

The covered shopping square with shops and bar

Partially open cupboards were the partitions between the classrooms in the schools

A main column with parasol-truss as skylight

Applied Mathematics and Computing Centre University of Twente Enschede

Leo Heijdenrijk and Jos Mol *Design 1970 Realization 1971–1973*

In a preliminary study by Heijdenrijk and Mol an inventory was made of the possibilities for a complex of faculty buildings for Applied Mathematics with a computing centre, Social Sciences and Electrical Engineering. In order to maintain the landscape character of the country estate of Drienerlo it was decided in favour of low-rise. The basic principle was a structure of strips of building which were constructed from 'building blocks'. It was also attempted to interweave the buildings with the existing water. The building blocks were constructed from a core for vertical traffic with a work/lecture hall and staff rooms on a continuous horizontal corridor. The lower building remained mostly open and on the first floor the corridor formed an inner street as access for the various strips of buildings at right angles to it. In this layout the faculties could be built in different phases and extension of each strip of buildings remained a possibility. By using a small-scale measurement system, where bays could be left out at some points if needed, it was easy to react to landscape elements which were to be preserved.

In the definitive brief a part of the accepted plan was developed and realised. The building for the faculty of Applied Mathematics with a computing centre is partly in the water and is linked to the other side by a bridge for pedestrians and cyclists. The construction was built in concrete poured on the spot, with parts like the beams being prefabricated. Parapets and closed wall sections are built inside and outside in grey concrete blocks. The walls acquire a striking, almost brutalist expression through use of a fixed sunshade of prefabricated concrete components around the rows of windows.

The concrete skeleton is based on strips of building with columns in the wall zones and a row of eccentrically positioned intermediate columns. For each 'building block', there were two U-shaped central cores with stairs, lifts, cloakroom and toilets. As the floor plans show, the skeleton was rather freely manipulated by leaving out bays at some points to the side of the central corridor. Building volumes have been added and left out at the ends of the strips to avoid dead corners.

The exterior has a complicated character in which the various functions can hardly be identified because of the striking presence of the sunshades. Because of the free interpretation of the skeleton the interior is a lightly organised chain of classrooms and staff rooms, with the central facilities such as library and canteen on the inner street on the first floor.

Preliminary study of a considerably larger complex of faculty buildings than was ultimately realised for the same site in Drienerlo

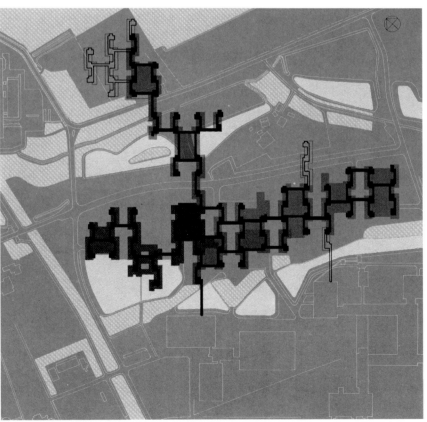

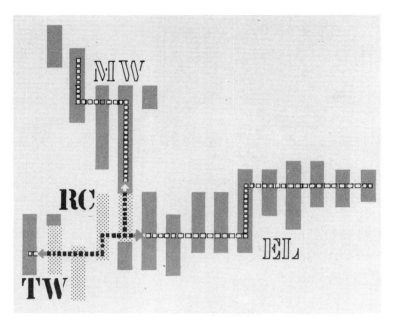

Elaboration of the structural design

MW Social Sciences
RC Computer Centre
TW Applied Physics
EL Electrical Engineering

First floor and cross section

1 seminar room
2 lecture hall
3 meeting room
4 courtyard
5 library
6 stairs
7 cloakroom / toilet
8 reception
9 canteen
10 kitchen
11 lift
12 installations
13 void computer room
14 waiting room
15 traffic room
16 roof

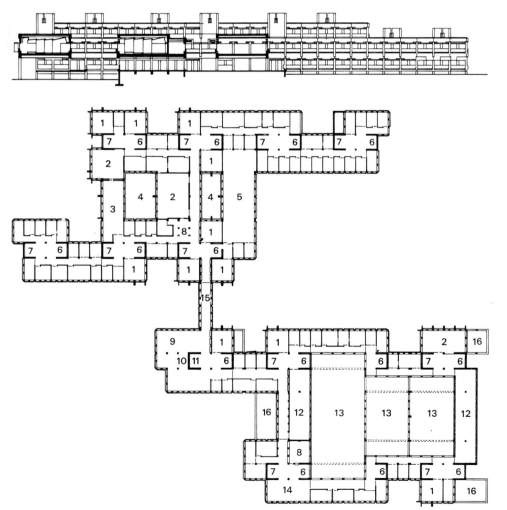

Junction of corridors with a stairway

Nursing home De Drie Hoven Amsterdam-Slotervaart

Herman Hertzberger *Commission 1965 Design and realization 1971–1974*

The nursing home De Drie Hoven contains 55 dwellings for couples, 171 housing units for 190 people and a nursing home with 250 beds for the long-term sick and senile elderly people, with rooms holding up to four people. In the heart of the building is an encounter centre around a covered courtyard. Around this central building there are various wings with a large part of the rooms on either sides of the central corridor. The building height varies from two to five floors.

The constructive structure consists of fourteen rigid cores with stairwells and lifts. Between them a prefabricated skeleton has been placed consisting of columns with two, three or four consoles on which rest joists with TT floor slabs. The basic principle was a module of 0.92 metres which occurs in the skeleton in multiples of 1.84, 2.76, 3.68 metres. The floor plan of the inner courtyard shows how the main layout is based on a grid of 3.68, which has been freely manipulated at the junctions with the wings, so that smaller distances are also to be found.

The inner walls are built in clean masonry of concrete blocks, also the rooms of the residents. The entrance to the housing units are on broadenings of the corridor, often beside a column, creating transitional areas between hall and housing. Hertzberger used half-doors which made it possible for the residents to have the door to the outside world partly open.

The square on the first floor of the centre building has a void to the second floor with a big skylight above it. Here too there is a chain of different spaces, some with low walls which you can sit on or put things on. Residents who use this space can choose between a sheltered spot on the lower periphery or a more communal one under the big void of this covered court.

The outer walls consist mainly of wooden facades with jambs and rails coloured dark green, with some lighter coloured panels. Depending on the orientation to the sun and use of the interiors the facades are filled in with glass or closed panels. The glass walls are also used at the loggias and roof terraces.

This big nursing home has therefore been approached as a city within the city, as a compensation for the inhabitants who cannot go outside very easily. The garden with various semi-open courts is also accessible to inhabitants of the neighbourhood around the nursing home. The paths under the building are a part of the pedestrian routes in the neighbourhood.

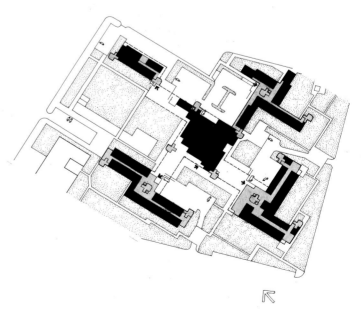

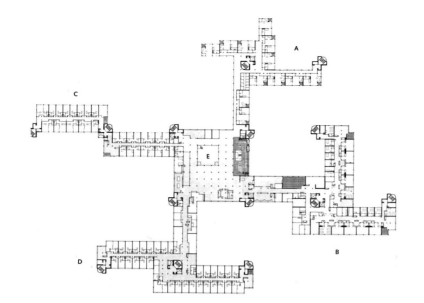

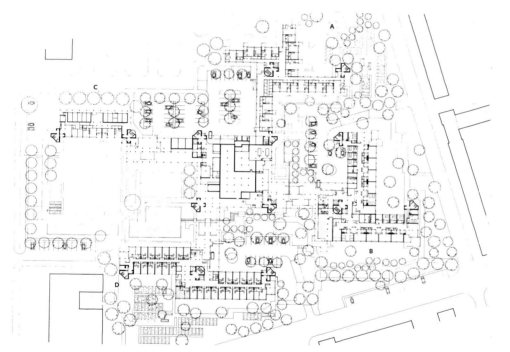

The building around the three open courts shortly after the building was opened

At some points the open
roof terrace acquires
conservatory-like covering

The ground floor has been left open at some points

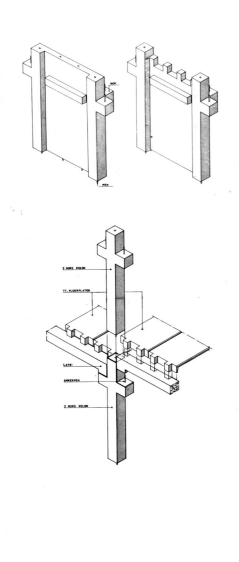

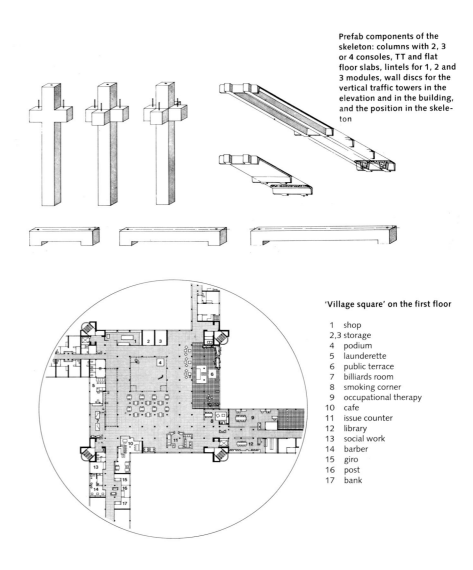

Prefab components of the skeleton: columns with 2, 3 or 4 consoles, TT and flat floor slabs, lintels for 1, 2 and 3 modules, wall discs for the vertical traffic towers in the elevation and in the building, and the position in the skeleton

'Village square' on the first floor

1   shop
2,3 storage
4   podium
5   launderette
6   public terrace
7   billiards room
8   smoking corner
9   occupational therapy
10 cafe
11 issue counter
12 library
13 social work
14 barber
15 giro
16 post
17 bank

Social Services and dwellings Leeuwarden

Abe Bonnema *Design 1972 Realization 1973–1975*

The office building for the Social Services in Leeuwarden is located on a site which became free in the facade of the Vliet, which had been filled in, immediately outside the old centre. The building has a height of two to three floors and is flanked on both sides by housing.

Bonnema was looking for a prefabricated skeleton which would be efficient for building in the inner city. The basis is a smallscale grid which fits in with the scale of the surroundings. The top floor was given the form of interrupted gable roofs. The flat roofs are flanked by roof sides with tiles at right angles to the facade.

The dwellings are hardly eight metres deep. The office building has a depth of about thirty metres and is built around a cruciform patio, around which the office spaces are arranged in the form of terraces.

For the facade, the concrete skeleton, visible both inside and outside, has been filled in with glass fronts, prefabricated parapets of concrete and at some points clean red brick masonry. The skeleton is based on two module of 2.5 x 2.5 metres and 5.0 x 5.0 metres, which are freely interpreted with regard to each other. The columns show a strong standardization with four poured consoles in which a groove is included on all sides for possible joining of fronts, walls or brickwork, also while the building is in use. On the consoles rest beams with the floors on them. For the roof constructions too this skeleton has been logically applied. The skeleton makes it easy to realise alterations as well as extensions if required.

The ground floor has an entrance which is displaced inward. The hall for visitors has been treated as an inner courtyard with 'street furniture and glass fronts' which alternate with clean brickwork. The roof terraces are provided with plant pots designed by the landscape architect Mien Ruys.

Patio, back garden and roof terraces show a varied reciprocity between interior and exterior

Detached house Retie, Belgium

Aldo van Eyck *Design and realization 1974–1975*

Commissioned by Mr G.J. Visser, Aldo van Eyck designed a detached house in a suburb of Retie. On the corner site in the wooded surroundings the one-storey dwelling
stands in an open space among the greenery.

The house, with an external size of 16.6 x 14.04 metres, is built completely in wood.
The skeleton os based on a square of 4.6 metres which is bevelled off at the corners.
In some places this square is enlarged into a rectangle. These basic components are
separate from each other, at a distance of 1.41 metres, which led to a square-like
interior being created in the heart of the dwelling. Two octagonal skylights have been
placed at the intersections of the space between the basic forms and ensure that the
daylight penetrates deeply into the dwelling, diagonally through the court. The two
squares on this diagonal in the corners are covered exterior spaces. In this way a
'bunch of places' was created with a limited repertoire of bevelled squares and rectangles: the entrances are deep in the building volume under the skylights, one being
within and the other outside the boundary of the dwelling space. The double columns
on the bevelled corners created two octagonal intermediate spaces as spatial transitions.

At the back, a circular fence ensures a more closed outside space between dwelling
and shed. The dwelling has a wooden skeleton with raised roof floors above the
basic components of squares and rectangles. The shed links up with this in layout
and details.

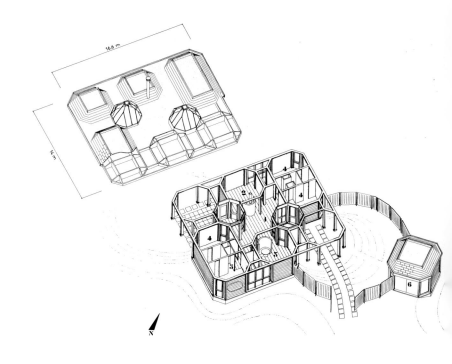

Street side, with on the left the palings around a more private outside area

Isometry

1 living room
2 sitting room
3 kitchen
4 bedroom
5 bathroom
6 storage

The spatial transition from exterior to interior through a covered outside area with roof structure

Interior under a roof structure

Library Doetinchem

Wim Davidse *Design 1970–1972 Realization 1975–1976*

The detached library in Doetinchem is at the edge of the inner city between a series of existing villas and a block of shops with dwellings above them. In awarding the commission much emphasis was laid upon the inviting character; a visit to the library should mean more than selecting a book. As well as the various departments for the library and the staff the programme of requirements also mentioned a coffee corner, a reading room for magazines, lending room for art and music and a space for diverse meetings.

The concrete construction, poured on the spot, has a freely interpreted construction grid of ten by ten metres, consisting of columns with beams and floors. At the edges of the building the columns are included in the construction of the wall area, with sections like stairs under sloping glass roofs built entirely in concrete. The skeleton of the walls is filled in with wooden facades from floor to roof and concrete bricks. Concrete was also used for the centrally positioned skylights. Originally the design had two of these skylights, with the form of sail arms. Retaining walls and seating walls with plant pots ensure a good transition from the building to the immediate surroundings. The entrances displaced inward are under awnings which serve as terraces on the first floor.

The central void under the skylight allows the daylight to penetrate deeply into the building and also ensures plentiful visual contact between visitors on the ground floor and the first floor.

The roofs of coloured wooden slats are attached within the end beams of the floor, through which the construction structures the space in size and scale. Much attention is devoted to the finish of the hardwood facades, balustrades around the void and stairs, the lending desk and the magazines reading room, as a contrast to the rough concrete poured on the spot.

The low garden walls and brick
flower boxes 'embed' the library
in its immediate surroundings

Ground floor			First floor		
1	entrance	9 toilets		15 lending for young people	23 toilets
2	enclosed porch	10 lift		16 reading store	24 pantry
3	lending for adults	11 service entrance		17 void	25 store
4	sitting/conversation area	12 terrace		18 discotheque	26 lift
5	lending centre	13 ramp		19 hall	27 to plant
6	reading room	14 pavement		20 lecture room	28 hall
7	study room			21 storage	29 director
8	cloakroom			22 roof terrace	30 staff cloakroom
					31 book maintenance
					32 administration

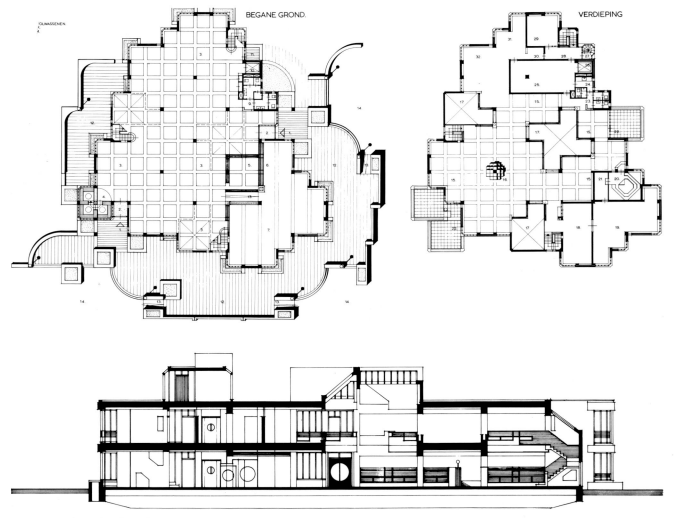

Cross section of central void and plant room on the roof

Central void

The library
from the
magazines
reading room

Town hall Lelystad
Leo Heijdenrijk *Design 1977*

After an extensive selection procedure, with architects being invited via an advertisement to reply if interested, a multiple commission was awarded to Jan Hoogstad – whose design was built – Jón Kristinsson and Leo Heijdenrijk (Environmental Design). The design by Heijdenrijk was notable for its structuralist approach. He himself characterised his design as 'A house like a city: a town hall', in which the administrative centre was regarded as the heart of the city centre. Along the edges of the town hall shops, kiosks and restaurants were envisaged as a transition from the surroundings to the civic square. To one side of this public space was the council hall as a space which was easily accessible to the public. The various departments of the town hall were within a grid of inner streets situated at right angles to each other. The building height varied from one to three floors, covered with sloping glass roofs, which also covered inner streets and city square.

The construction consisted of floor areas of 12.6 to 12.6 metres, with between them the inner streets of 5.4 metres, which were diagonally situated. The smallest module was 1.8 metres. Once again Leo Heijdenrijk shows how structuralists treat the chosen configuration and accompanying construction in a free manner. In the space between the floor areas voids were included, but floors were also continued at some points; at the intersections stairs were sometimes situated, but these could also be placed on the exterior. At the edges of the floor area projections were possible but also extensions with two extra columns which would lead to big diagonally placed extensions.

The facades were given numerous transitions in sloping glass roofs and together with the diagonally-placed extensions produced a 'soft exterior' which assumed expressive forms. In the commentary on the design, Heijdenrijk referred to the Viennese 'Stadt des Kindes' by Anton Schweighofer, a photo of which was included in the presentation book. As materials for the walls he chose brick with wooden fronts and wall frames as sunshade; sloping closed wall zones would be covered with copper.

In its main layout Leo Heijdenrijk's design had much in common with his design for the Amsterdam town hall, even though the complicated mushroom-style construction with beam grid has been exchanged for a beamless floor construction. The free interpretation of this construction, especially at the wall edges, made the structure considerably more complicated than the town hall design on the Amstel.

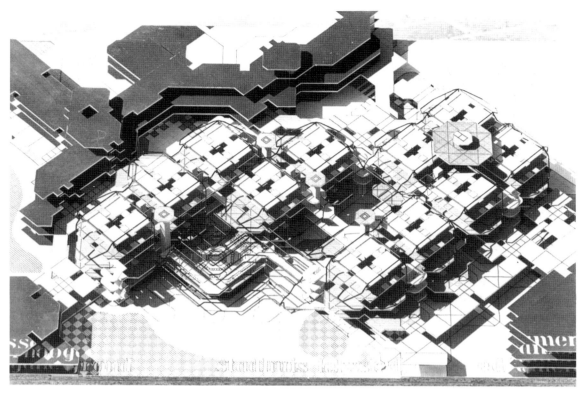

Maquette of town hall with adjacent buildings

Detail of Stadt des Kindes in Vienna (1974) by Anton Schweighofer which was quoted by Heijdenrijk as a reference point for the architecture he advocated

Interior of a passageway

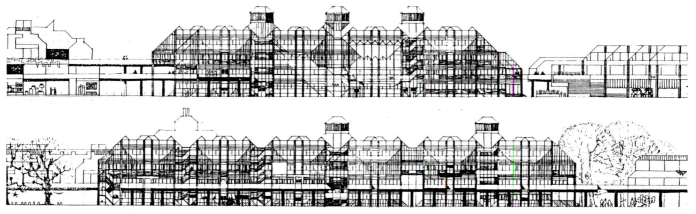

Southeast and southwest elevation

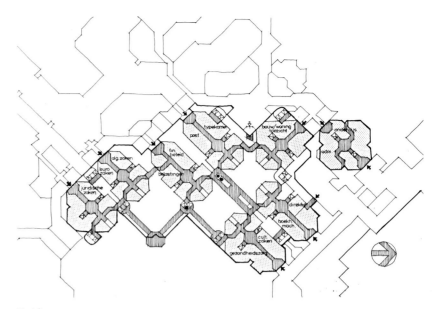

First floor

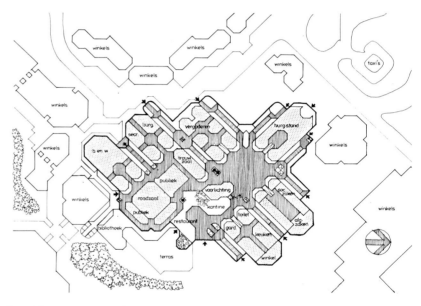

Ground floor

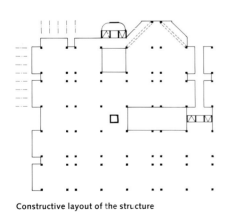

Constructive layout of the structure

Cultural centre De Flint Amersfoort

Onno Greiner *Design 1966–1975 Realization 1975–1977*

The design for a multi-functional cultural centre at the edge of the old centre of Amersfoort was completed in 1974 after many changes and a far-reaching minimalization. The basic principles were versatility, smallness of scale and integration of activities.

Central to the design are two inner streets which meet at a T-junction and on which are situated the various functions within the complex. De Flint has a theatre for five hundred people, a city hall where about a thousand people can come together, a creative centre which is suitable for all kinds of activities and a bar-restaurant.

In his design Onno Greiner was looking for an adaption in size, scale and material with regard to the inner city. Because the programme of requirements stipulated many spaces with a floor surface of forty square metres, or multiples of this, Greiner applied a basic pattern of 6.4 x 6.4 metres, which linked up well with the average plot width in the inner city. In this, the design formed a picture at a given moment in time, 1970, of the required spaces, which in the course of time could simply be extended by new building.

The construction was based on a simple concrete skeleton which was standardised and prefabricated as much as possible. The walls were built around the skeleton in masonry with window frames, analogous to the traditional brick architecture in the surroundings. The building height varies from one to two floors with a few high building volumes at some points, in which the structure of squares in the floor plan recurs. These building volumes are covered with small prefabricated pyramidic roofs of timber with brown asphalt slates. The construction remained visible everywhere inside the complex, also in the roofs. The inner streets, with walls of clean masonry and paving of clinkers and concrete tiles have retained the character of inner city streets and are semi-public.

Around ten years after the building was opened, it has turned out to be so successful that extension is desirable. It is even being considered moving it, which has met with much resistance from the residents of the neighbourhood of De Teut.

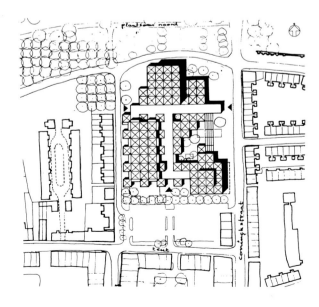

Gently sloping pyramidic roofs make a structure of squares in the plan clearly visible

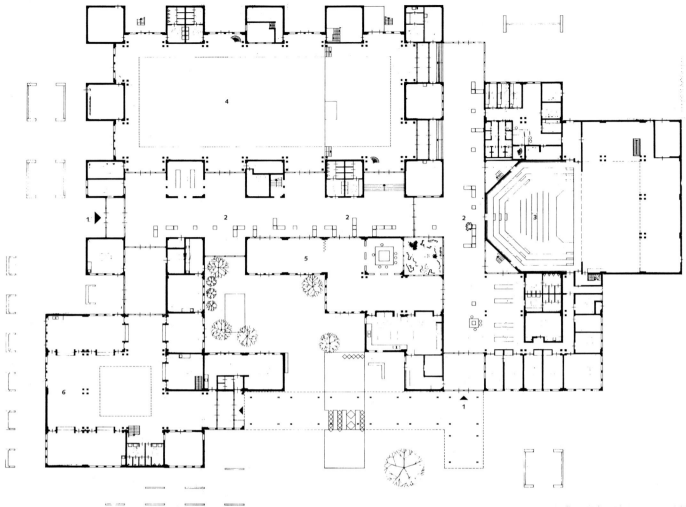

Floor plan

1 entrance
2 inner street
3 theatre hall
4 city hall
5 café/restaurant
6 hall of creative centre

Inner street broadening at some
points into small squares

City hall during
an exhibition

Hall of creative centre

Stadthalle Biberach an der Riss, Germany

Onno Greiner *Design 1971–1973 Realization 1974–1977*

The city council of the Southern German city of Biberach an der Riss in Baden-Württemberg set a competition in 1970 for the design of a town hall as a multi-functional cultural centre. Because Onno Greiner's cultural centre De Tamboer in Hoogeveen appealed to the preparatory committee, he was one of the four foreign architects invited and won the first prize.

The competition design from 1971 underwent profound changes. For example, the multi-functional use was reduced to the concentration of possible activities in a single space. The original pattern of 8.5 x 8.5 metres was therefore sharply reduced.

The Stadthalle is just outside the old centre of the city on a sloping site at the foot of the Gigelberg. The building is partly sunk into the site and has five different floor levels; the main level is seven metres above the street. At the centre there is a theatre hall which in its maximum form, including surrounding rooms made available by sliding walls, can contain twelve hundred people. It also has a smaller hall, a restaurant, rooms for an adult education centre, a bar and skittle alleys.

The construction is based on a grid of squares, 6 x 6 metres, which are positioned just separate from each other. Because each square has its own columns at the corners, clusters of four free-standing columns were created, between which sliding walls disappear at some points. Around larger spaces, the four columns are joined into a single heavy column. The independence of the loadbearing construction for each unit made it simple to realise the various floor levels within the building against the mountain slope.

The concrete construction was made on the spot. The walls are finished in slabs of lightly-coloured prefabricated concrete which link up with the traditional plastered facades in the surroundings. The light pyramid-shaped roofs are of timber and were delivered prefabricated. They are faced with copper on the exterior and finished with wooden laths on the inside.

The design for the Stadthalle was created at almost the same time as the definitive design for De Flint in Amersfoort. A related approach can be found in the floor plans, the working with squares which ultimately became about the same size in the two buildings. The budget for Biberach was considerable higher than in Amersfoort, which made a considerably higher level of finish possible. This was expressed in the cubic metre price which was seventy five per cent higher than in Amersfoort.

End wall

The building at the foot of the Gigelberg

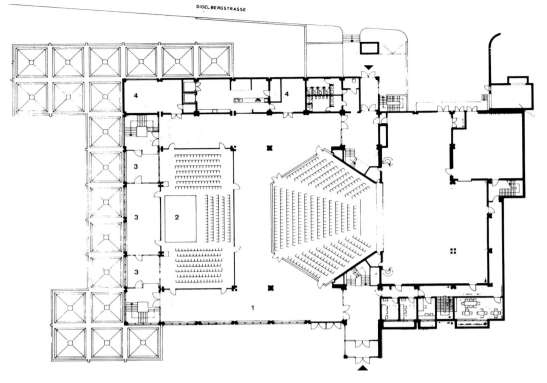

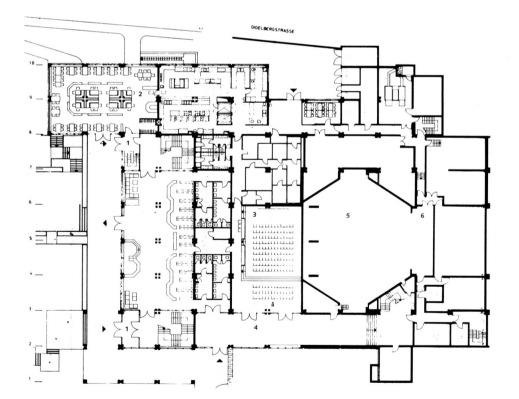

Central hall

Restaurant

College Delft
Hendriks, Campman and Tennekes *Design 1974 Realization 1976–1977*

The building for the Southwest Holland Teachers' Training College, on the border between Delft and Rijswijk was in the first instance intended for 2,500 students and can easily be extended.

The building, with two and sometimes three floors, is constructed on a two-sided grid of 5.4 metres. 'Towers' of 27 x 27 metres (5 modules) whose squares are left out at the corners, were also used; this created cross-shaped building sections. This cruciform is connected in such a way that each of them is one module removed from the other with a stairway between them. Three groups of four crosses surround three inner courts which are roofed by a girder frame.

The cruciform floors rest on two round columns per side in the edge zone and four central columns. The concrete construction has coffer floors which were poured on the spot. Access to the classrooms and so on takes place along the central axes, continuations of landings which link up with the semi-circular concrete stairwells. Toilets and storage are at the heart of the cruciform floors.

The filling in of these floors with the help of moveable walls turned out to be suitable for extremely diverse layouts. For two lecture halls which required more space the recessed corners were simply left out.

A part of the building has remained open on the ground floor and stands on 'pilotis' with entrance and bicycle racks between the columns, among other things. The entrance is therefore set somewhat inward, thus accompanying the transition from exterior to interior. You then come out on the 'agora', the central covered court on which a series of communal facilities are situated on the ground floor and first floor, such as the canteen, lecture halls and library. Daylight enters through roof structures along the edges of the roof.

The walls consist of facades which are partly closed and are a half-module wide. These facades run on the outside along the columns which are set somewhat back. The aim is to have as much glass as possible in the receding corners, thus emphasising a diagonal effect with lines of sight to other parts of the complex.

The development of structural layout, contents and details is often on the dry side, but gives the whole a high level of clarity within the overall complex. The complex in Delft is now being used as a component of the Rotterdam and Region Hogeschool.

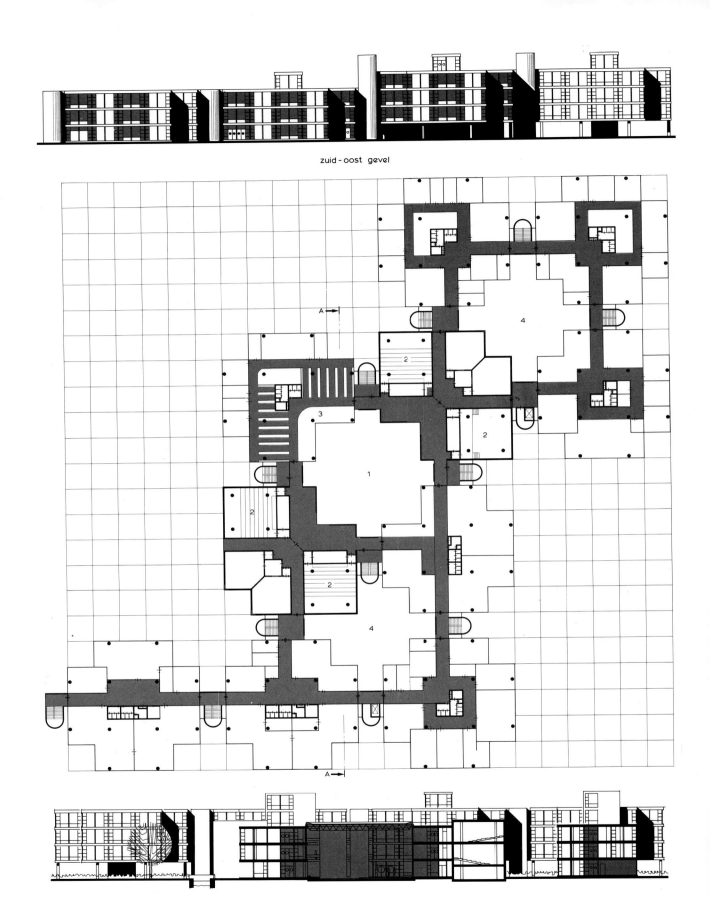

zuid - oost gevel

First floor with A-A cross section and southeast elevation

1   agora
2   seminar rooms
3   library
4   inner courtyard

The agora across a diagonal with the restaurant on the ground floor

Hubertushuis Amsterdam
Aldo van Eyck *Design and realization 1973–1978*

The Hubertushuis, also called the Mothers' House, is a centre for single parents who need temporary shelter and/or guidance. On average they spend six months at the Hubertushuis, which has a capacity for 16 parents, mainly mothers, and 78 children. The building consists of two parts: a new building and a renovated and adapted historic house. Staff and parents are housed in the existing building, the children, kitchen and eating area are housed in the new building.

The new building has a concrete skeleton for a total of six floors; the main floor is partly connected to the existing building and partly somewhat higher, split-level-style, above a lower floor. Behind, on an inner site there is a low building section with living and sleeping accommodation for children from 1 to 6 years.

The lowrise is traditionally built to a great extent. The higher building at the front has a concrete skeleton whose bay widths at right angles to the facade are all different and become smaller in the direction of the old building. Depth-wise too, the columns are at different distances from each other. From the second floor the concrete skeleton in the bay against the old building becomes a light steel construction. The floor heights in this bay link up with the higher floors of the old building; the two broadest bays contain compacted floors which are partly connected to the other floors, split-level-style. The stairwell is housed in the remaining bay; for the lowest floors the stairs are on the street side, higher up the stairs are at the back with a view of the department for young children. The seven stairs which have been fitted here, are all different from each other in form.

One seldom encounters a concrete skeleton which has been so strongly manipulated and made subordinate to the spatial wishes: almost all bays are different in size and have various heights in the split-level style floors. As well as this, extremely diverse terrace forms have been used, both in the facade and rear. Outer and inner walls are to a great extent left transparent, with the stairwell forming a highpoint in the transparent building volume.

The spatial layout is strongly reminiscent of the 'bunches of places' championed by Van Eyck, in which surprising elements are to be found such as the main entrance in the old building and the strong relationship of the various building sections with each other. For the first time, Van Eyck here uses on a very large scale, his 'favourite colour, the rainbow', both inside and outside the building.

Overview and detail of the facade

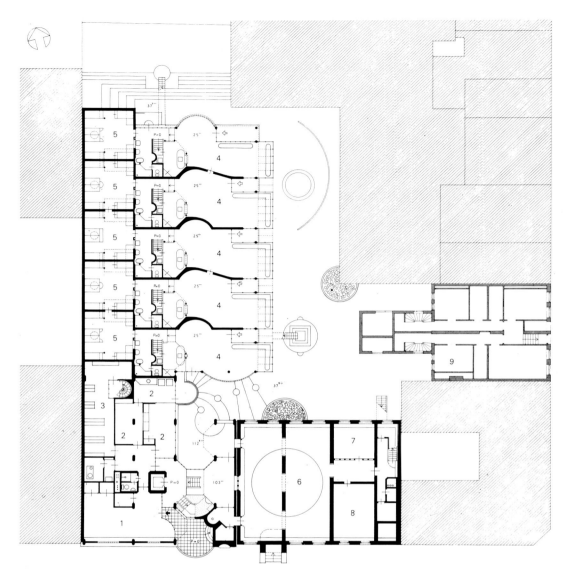

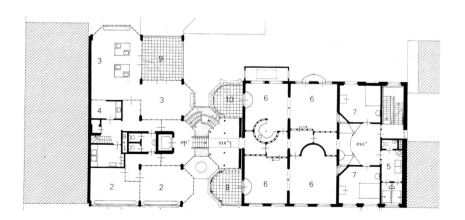

Ground floor (above)

1 bicycles, prams
2 laundry and linen-room
3 pantry
4 living rooms
   children 1-6 years
5 sleeping quarters
6 games room
7 workshop
8 storage
9 sold

Second floor

1 hall
2 workrooms
3 babies
4 kitchen
5 scullery
6 parents' living rooms
7 parents' bedrooms
8 bathroom
9 loggia
10 roof terrace

The stairwell is like a bunch of
linked spaces

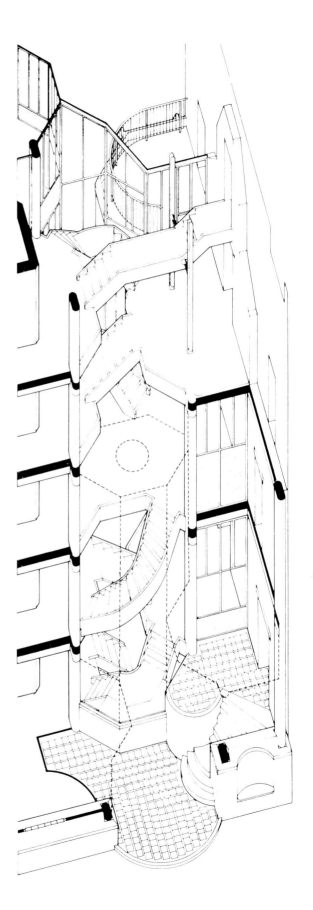

Muziekcentrum Vredenburg Utrecht

Herman Hertzberger *Preliminary design 1969–1971 Design 1973–1976 Realization 1976–1979*

At the preliminary design phase of the music centre, Hertzberger emphasised the transition from the new, large-scale complex Hoog Catharijne to the old city centre. A planned traffic route made way, after prolonged discussions, for the Vredenburg square. The final design consisted of a concert hall for 1700 people, a small hall for 350 people with adjoining accommodation and shops, bars and restaurants on two floors on an arcade.

Although the design is based on a prefabricated concrete construction with a grid of 3 x 6 metres, a construction poured on the spot with round columns and a two-sided grid of six metres turned out to be more efficient. The columns with a diameter of 47 centimetres were given a square column plate or 'capital', which made then somewhat bigger than was necessary for the construction. Along the edges on the street facades there are deviations from the pattern. At some places there are columns two floors high while the steel roof construction of the big hall is apparently resting on standard columns, but these have considerably heavier reinforcement.

The skeleton is filled in mainly with glass facades with vertical forms and masonry of concrete blocks, which were specially made for this job. The block height of 167 millimetres plus a horizontal point is equal to the height of one step. In a separate drawing Hertzberger shows a great number of various joining possibilities of glass and brickwork in this column form, to make clear the potential possibilities and the freedom within the skeleton.

This repertoire of the visible skeleton with clean masonry and glass bays is supplemented by railings, balustrade components and steel awnings. What is striking is the way some fragments of historic buildings have been fitted in. Parts of the monastery dating from around 1200 and the castle Vredenburg from the sixteenth century which were discovered when digging the foundations have been fitted into the cellar of the Tourist Information Office and on the exterior, often on the original location. Jugendstil railings and postbox from the demolished head office of De Utrecht and a caryatid by Mendes da Costa from the archives building were reused by Hertzberger. These fragments reminiscent of the earlier building and history of this site have been effortlessly included in Hertzberger's architecture.

The music centre is situated in the middle of the shopping district

First floor

1 main hall
2 podium
3 skylight

4 foyer of main hall
5 snackbar
6 small hall
7 foyer of small hall
8 exhibition space

9 lift
10 cloakroom
11 Tourist Information Office
12 Muziekcentrum offices
13 shop

14 restaurant
15 office
16 passageway
17 terrace
18 connection with Hoog Catharijne

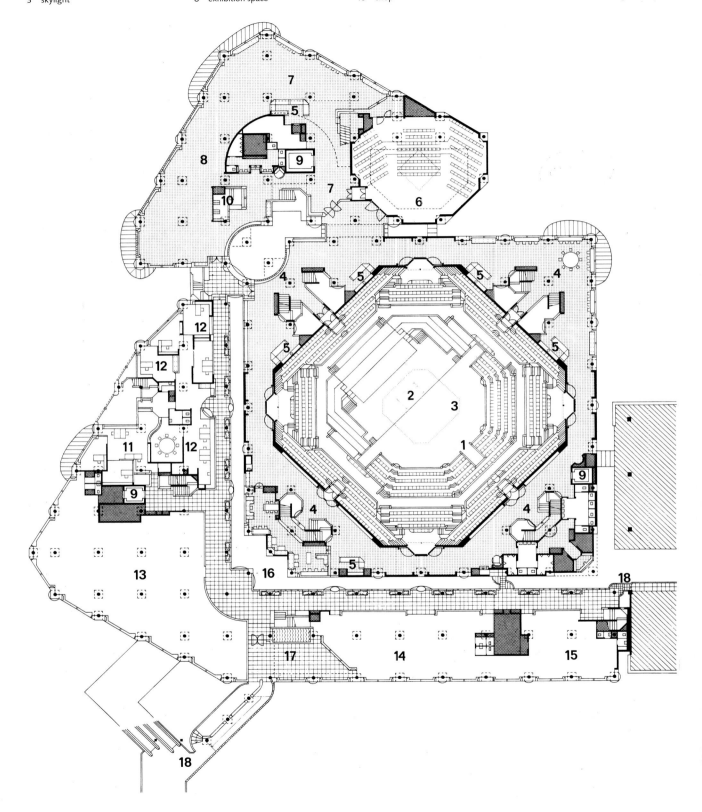

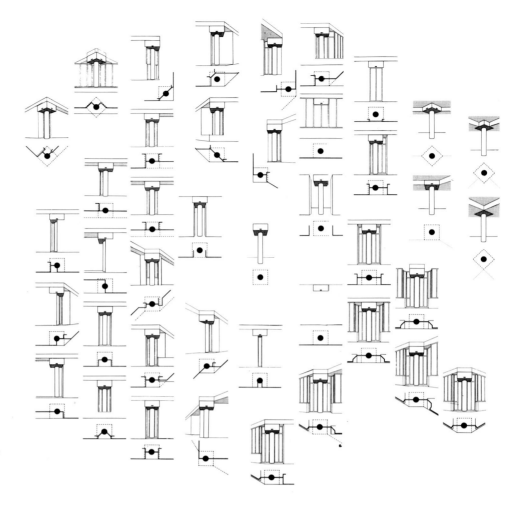

Diverse positions of
standard columns with
connections to walls and
facades

Cross section of the passageway at the main entrance to
the big hall

Example of diverse connections
to two wall columns

The passageway

Alternating spatial relations
in the foyers

The main hall of the music centre

Faculty buildings and library University of Leiden

Joop van Stigt and Bart van Kasteel *Design 1976–1978 Realization 1979–1982*

After P. Zanstra's 1971 design for the Alpha faculties was hit by a building freeze, the 125-metres-high tower vanished into a drawer. At the end of 1975 commissions were given to five architects for smaller buildings. Joop van Stigt designed two faculty complexes with a library by Bart van Kasteel between them, on a site on the outer side of the Witte Singel.

For the communal car park under the faculty buildings and the book cellar of two floors a similar construction was used: a mushroom-floor on a two-sided grid of 7.2 metres. This pattern also turned out to be suitable for the two faculty buildings and the library. Here, Joop van Stigt used a configuration of building parts with two squares of 14.4 metres which overlapped each other for a quarter; four of such building parts are located around a courtyard and on the larger scale are once again linked into two squares which partly overlap. Streets between these building sections have the width of a single bay or half of it which means that the pattern is interrupted by a narrow strip. This layout makes it possible to allow the various routes to penetrate all parts of the site with alternating smaller courtyards and larger square-type spaces at the margins.

Bart van Kasteel used the same columns and pattern of size but filled them in differently with covered halls instead of courtyards. The streets are partly to be found again in the library as access routes within the building.

For the walls Joop van Stigt used brick whereby the construction remained clearly visible as a structuring scale for the buildings in this inner city location. The roof construction is built in wood and is reminiscent of the staff canteen in Drienerlo and the town hall in Ter Aar.

Bart van Kasteel chose to face the walls in light-coloured stone which also remains bright in rainy weather and at some points, prefabricated concrete. On the ground floor the mushroom columns – without any finish – are outside the outer wall; on the first floor bay-like additions have been placed around the columns and these are within the walls. The catalogue hall has a dome, both the other 'inner courtyards' have a glazed roof construction.

In this way a complex came into being which partly through the two different architectural approaches fits well into the urban fabric and as an interesting form of cooperation compares favourably with the simultaneously developed university buildings on the other side of the canal.

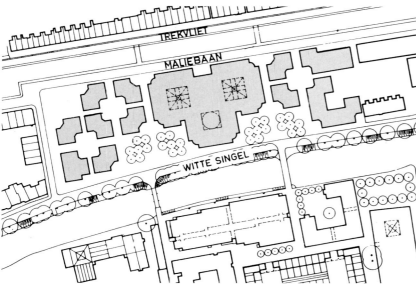

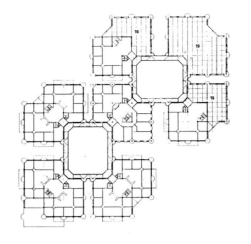
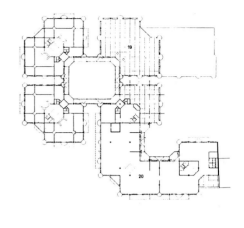

Ground floor of clusters by Van Stigt

1   English
2   Dutch
3   departmental library
4   German
5   departmental library
6   coffee room
7   caretaker
8   French
9   departmental library
10 Italian and Spanish
11 departmental library
12 African and other departments
13 departmental library
14 Near East
15 Arabic, Persian, Turkish and others
16 Hebrew and others
17 Theology
18 Dutch lexicography
19 roof terrace
20 departmental library

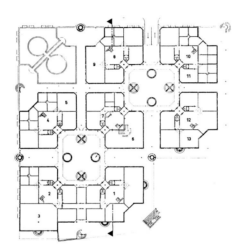

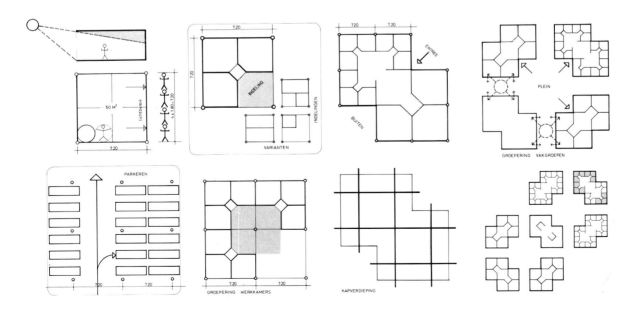

Structural layout
of Van Stigt's
design

The exterior of Joop van Stigt's faculty buildings

Ground floor of Bart van Kasteel's University Library

1	entrance	5	book lift
2	lift and stairwell	6	information desk
3	central hall	7	cloakroom
4	lending office	8	canteen

9 exhibition room
10 void to the cellar

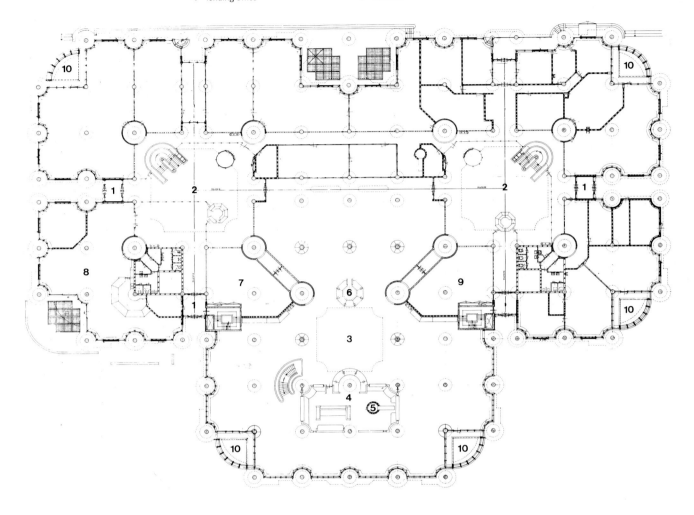

Elevations of Bart van
Kasteel's library

Covered courtyard
of the library

PEN offices Alkmaar

Abe Bonnema *Design 1977–1979 Realization 1979–1982*

The offices of the Provinciaal Elektriciteitsbedrijf Noord-Holland are on the edge of Alkmaar. The design had to include workshops and a car park as well as the office building. Because of the good impression made by his office building for the Social Services in Leeuwarden, commissioned by the staff, Abe Bonnema got the brief. The programme of requirements asked for a building which was not too large-scale, with a flexible layout, with overflow space for work areas on the floors, a sixty per cent saving in energy with regard to the then usual office buildings, the use of natural building materials and preferably sloping roofs.

This led to a sort of settlement on the edge of the meadow landscape, consisting of six building sections situated apart from each other around a green inner garden with water, and parking facilities at the periphery. Where necessary, the buildings are linked by bridges on the first floor. In this splitting up into different buildings, the architecture was meeting the demand for small-scale in the 1970s.

The construction is based on a two-sided grid of 7.2 metres for prefabricated columns with cast consoles on four sides. The roof floors, with partly sloping roofs are also constructed in this way. Prefabricated columns and beams have a corbel groove on four sides for simple joints with various wall constructions varying from closed brickwork to transparent facades. The concrete construction remained visible both inside and outside and is filled in with clean masonry of red brick, glass facades and roof shields which are covered in ceramic tiles. In order to allow in sufficient daylight vertical window strips have been applied which are supplemented by skylights at some spots.

The garden architects Mien Ruys were responsible for the plants on the roof terraces and laying out the inner garden and the immediate surroundings.

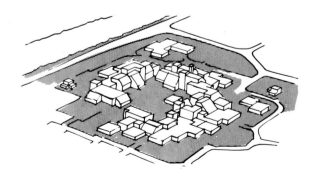

Overview of the inner garden with the North Holland landscape in the background

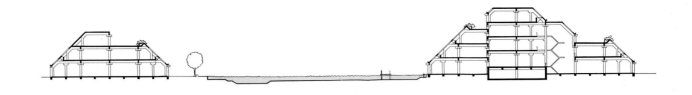

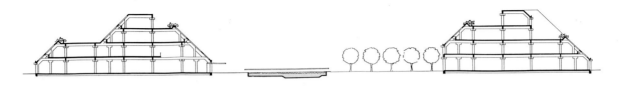

Two cross sections

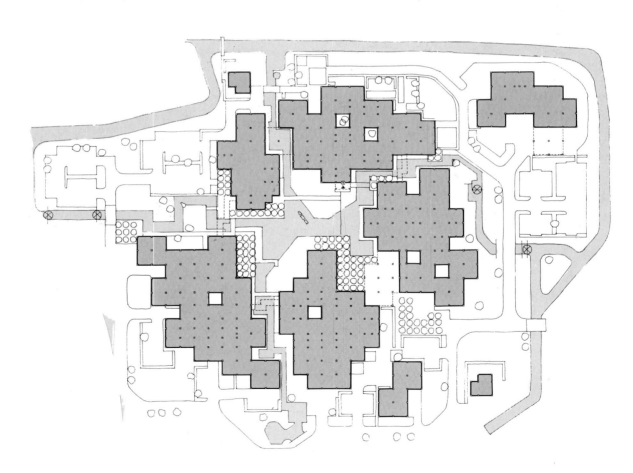

Plan of the complex. The mutual
connections of the buildings on the first
floor are indicated with a dotted line

**Detail with a bridge
on the first floor**

The complex in the landscape

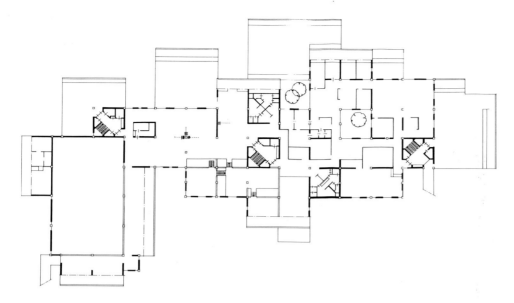

First floor of the main building

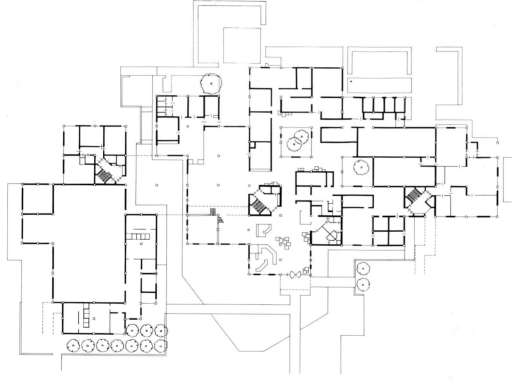

Ground floor of the main building

**Staggered levels
in the canteen**

Academic Medical Centre Amsterdam

Duintjer, Istha, Kramer and Van Willegen with D. van Mourik *Design 1968–1982 Realization 1975–1983*

The Amsterdam Academic Medical Centre is part of a series of new teaching hospitals, built to provide medical care, teaching and research. With 850 beds, an emergency capacity of 1200 extra beds and around 9000 users it is one of the biggest hospitals in the Netherlands. Because of the building process over many years it was necessary to phase the design: the layout of the various building sections was only designed in the structural work phase. Therefore the contents of the building had to be simple and continue to be alterable in building sections when in use. It also had to be possible to extend in the future.

The fundamental principle is a 'functional basic structure' with rows of departments alongside each other for internal medicine, surgery and neurology. On the other axis are situated outpatient clinics, research and treatment, staff and laboratories and research rooms. This led to a number of building sections in the lowrise which are separated from each other by inner streets at right angles to each other and larger squares under skylights. The vertical traffic with lifts and stairs is also included in this fabric of inner streets. In the main routes within the lowrise, bridges connect the buildings sections. Between these main routes then, depending on use, an increasingly finely-meshed system of corridors with adjacent rooms was created. The beds are housed in six towers which are placed, staggered with regard to each other, on either side of the central corridor. The emergency hospital is to one side of the lower building.

The construction consists of a concrete skeleton with columns on a two-sided grid of 7.8 metre. The height of the floors is extremely varied, with three plant floors being included in the lowrise, sandwich-style. In the floors above and below there are perforation zones to allow wiring through.

Just like the new teaching hospitals of Leiden and Groningen the hospital is certainly not a textbook example of structuralist architecture. But in the processing of the programme of requirements, in both the main structure and the desire for constant flexibility and possibilities for extension, a number of characteristics of structuralism can be recognised. In the exterior this intention was hardly present and this sometimes led to a utilitarian-looking facade.

Inner court with alternating work floors and lower installation floors

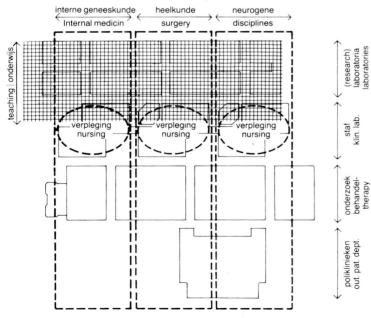

interne geneeskunde	heelkunde	neurogene
Internal medicin	surgery	disciplines

verpleging nursing verpleging nursing verpleging nursing

teaching onderwijs

(research) laboratoria laboratories

staf kiin. lab.

onderzoek behandel- therapy

poliklinieken out. pat. dept.

The functional basic structure for the Amsterdam Medical Centre

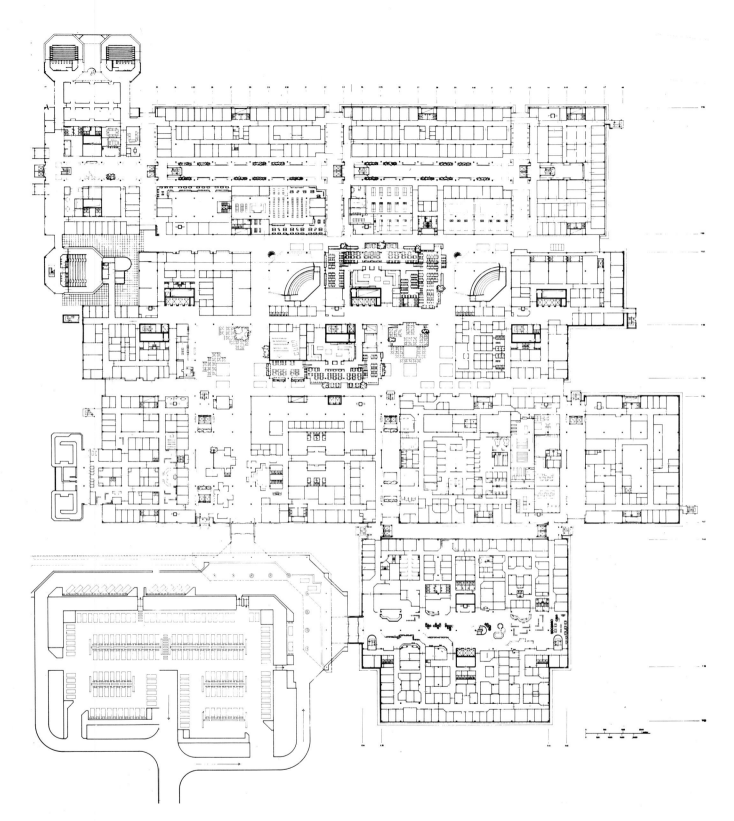

The main floor in the low-rise

Ministry of Education and Science Zoetermeer

Flip Rosdorff *Design 1975–1978 Realization 1980–1984*

The Ministry for around 2500 officials is at the edge of a residential district with single-family-dwellings and blocks of flats up to three storeys high, close to the new
centre of Zoetermeer. The acceptable building height was six to seven floors in the
heart of the site and considerably lower along the edges. Pedestrian routes over the
site in the direction of the shops and station were requested for the residents.
In building models a grid around square courtyards, detached buildings and loose
blocks was studied. The choice was for the blocks which were divided diagonally
into two hook-shaped wings. This gave the rooms a view of public space, but led
to a shortage of floor space. That shortage was solved with concentrations of octagonal towers at junctions and ending the building strips within the configuration
with L-shaped building sections. The octagons made it possible to deform the nine
L-shaped buildings sections with an inner corner of ninety to one hundred and thirty
five degrees.
The construction was built in concrete. For the straight building sections poured concrete was used with a span of 6.3 metres, derived from housing. The floors of the
octagons were borne by four round columns along the edges; where they were
joined pairs of columns with a shaft between for wiring were created. In the core of
the building which is surrounded by these octagons, lifts, stairs and at some points
voids are included.
Originally, a stone-like material was envisaged for the outer walls. Ultimately a grey
facade of aluminium was chosen with brick parapets around the ground level only.
The constructive round columns of the octagonal elements are recognizable through
interruption of the horizontal rows of windows. For maintenance, window-cleaner
balconies of steel have been fitted on the higher floors.
Within the building the construction has been left visible and hardly any lowered
ceilings have been fitted. Air ducts, cables and document transport have therefore
also been left visible.
In laying out the site the existing system of roads for pedestrians from the surroundings has been continued with adjoining green facilities, open spaces and parking
areas which outside office hours do not form empty car parks but rather small
squares. The underground infrastructure is recognizable in the finish of paving and
asphalting. The layout of the immediate surroundings of the building was designed
by landscape architect J. Boon.

The ministry for 2500 civil servants is located
in a small-scale residential neighbourhood

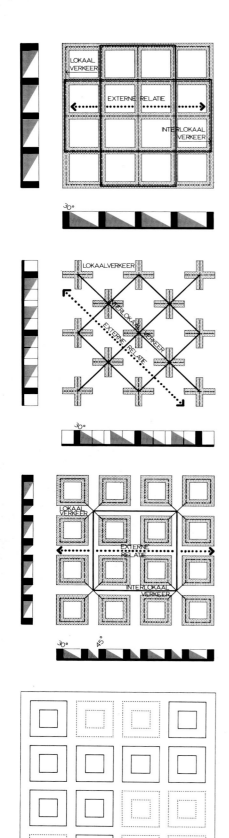

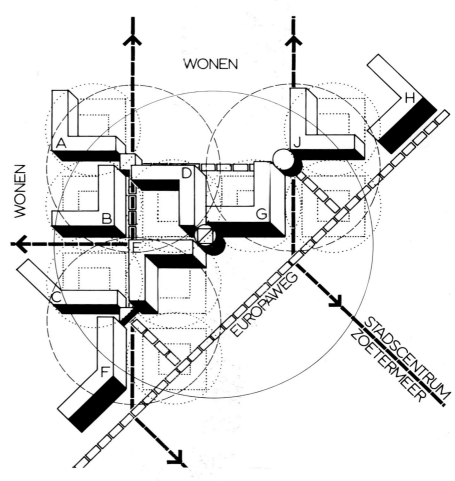

There were three different models consisting of buildings around sixteen courtyards, thirteen cruciform buildings and sixteen blocks. The last model was chosen, but leaving out seven blocks; by condensing the building height the remaining blocks could be manipulated into L-shaped buildings, and an open building structure with routes for local residents across the site

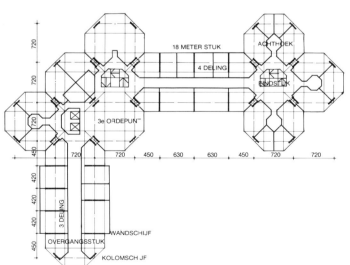

Partial floor plan with basic construction of round columns in the octagons and loadbearing cast-concrete walls in the straight wings

Street facade with long awning leading to the main entrance

Central junctions in the circulation spaces of the octagonal building sections

Gemäldegalerie Berlin
Herman Hertzberger *Design 1986*

Halfway through the 1960s Rolf Gutbrod was commissioned, after a competition, to design a complex with various museums for European art. Beside the Philharmonie by Hans Scharoun, Gutbrod designed the Kunstgewerbemuseum, the Kupferstich-kabinett and the Kunstbibliothek which would be built in phases with a shared entrance building. The Gemäldegalerie and Skulpturengalerie which were also included in the plan were not built according to Gutbrod's design. In 1986 a closed competition was set for the Gemäldegalerie, for which Herman Hertzberger was also invited. Hertzberger's design formed a painting landscape within an urban fabric of exhibition walls on a zigzag route for visitors. The visitor could shorten or interrupt his route by means of cross connections. A necessary difference of levels was included in a terrace-shaped floor construction.

Between the interrupted exhibition walls, extra walls, glass cases or sculptures could be placed if required. This led to a multi-functional exhibition landscape.

The construction consisted of columns which were included in the exhibition halls. Above the exhibition space in the roof construction a system of plant corridors was included which both provide space for the air conditioning plant and make it possible to transport paintings and lower them to the desired exhibition location through a transparent hatch. The plant corridors are linked directly to the painting depots along the street walls above the museum space. It formed a new structuralist interpretation of strongly differing building floors which are laid over each other like grids.

The entire exhibition space receives daylight through the roof, where the light intensity and temperature could be regulated. The walls of the installation corridors formed reflecting surfaces so that no direct sunlight would fall on the artworks. Hertzberger's design was striking in the completely new typology which it introduced for a museum with paintings. Two existing dwellings and the connection with the completed museum by Rolf Gutbrod were extra complications for this design task. The design was bought by the Stiftung Preussischer Kulturbesitz but has not been built.

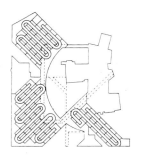
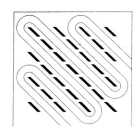
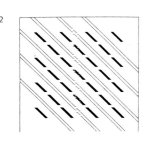

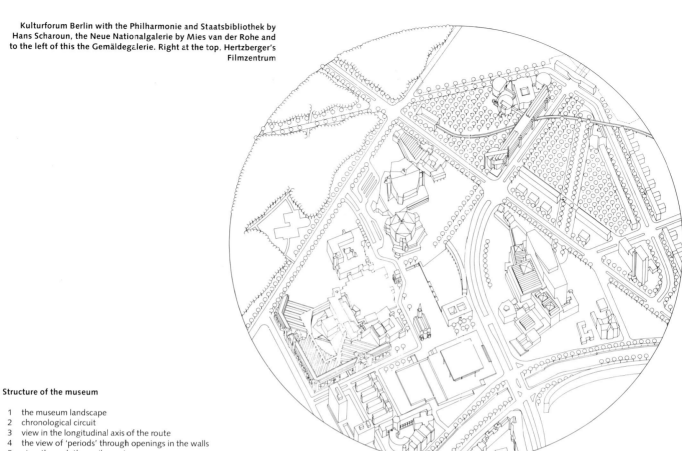

Kulturforum Berlin with the Philharmonie and Staatsbibliothek by Hans Scharoun, the Neue Nationalgalerie by Mies van der Rohe and to the left of this the Gemäldegalerie. Right at the top, Hertzberger's Filmzentrum

Structure of the museum

1   the museum landscape
2   chronological circuit
3   view in the longitudinal axis of the route
4   the view of 'periods' through openings in the walls
5   view through the wall openings
6   view at right angles to the main route
7   sub-division of exhibition spaces
8   exhibition panels against the walls
9   a wall opening as a passage
10   wall with display cases
11   natural light between plant corridors
12   sunlight entering

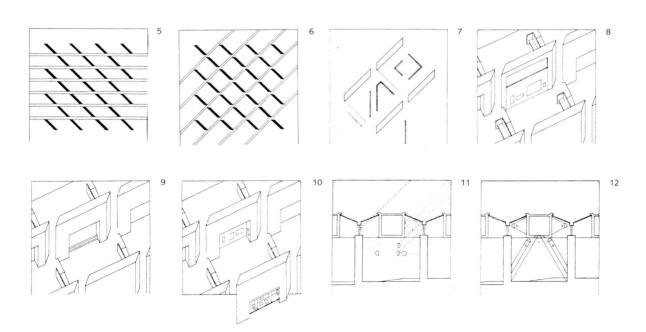

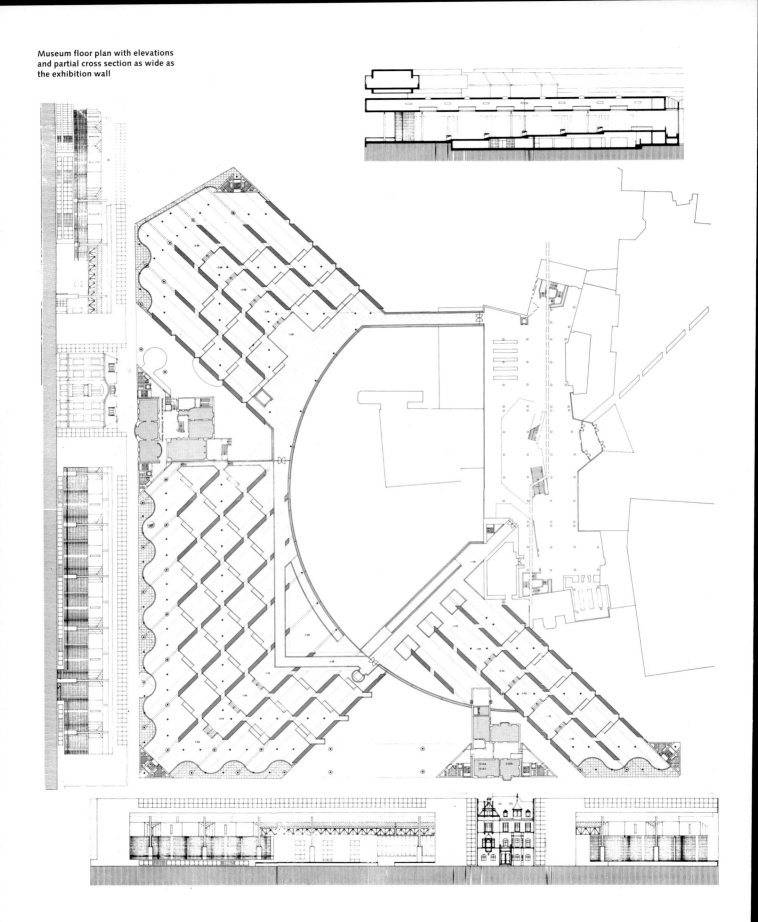

Museum floor plan with elevations
and partial cross section as wide as
the exhibition wall

Development of a fragment of the exhibition space

1   transparent glass
2   glass which can be added
3   movable plates
4   awning
5   plate 50% transparent and

     50% reflecting
6   light reflecting material
7   ventilation, extraction
8   ventilation, infusion
9   trolley

10   exhibition panel
11   seat
12   glass case
13   transport hatch

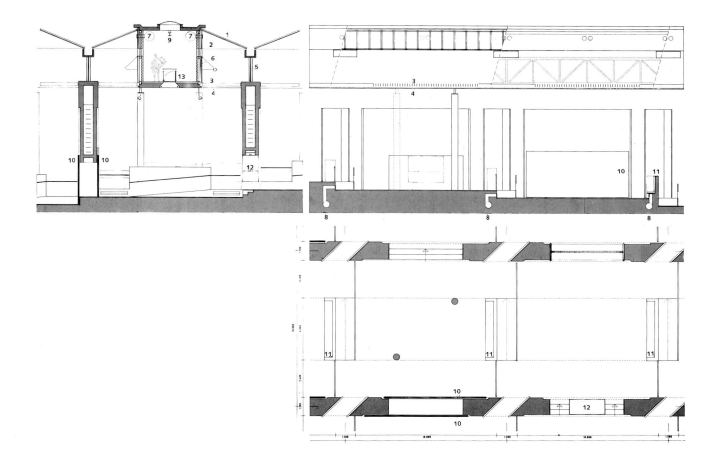

Bibliothèque de France Paris

Herman Hertzberger *Design 1989*

Within the context of a series of prestigious building projects by the French President Mitterand, a competition was set for a new building for the national library in Paris. A site on the Seine between the Bercy and Tolbiac bridges was set aside for the extremely large library. Twenty architects were invited to make a design, including Architectonica, Bofill, Botta, Koolhaas, Maki, Nouvel, Stirling and Hertzberger. Herman Hertzberger's design consisted of a platform rising in steps with parking facilities and technical facilities under it. The library space was envisaged as a single big central hall above the platform: a covered square with a glazed roof construction. In high transparent container-like building volumes different functions such as reference library, research libraries with reading rooms, an audiovisual library and children's books were housed. A peripheral construction of three floors which ran around the high glass roof of the central hall was envisaged (comparable to the painting depots in the design for the Gemäldegalerie in Berlin).

The construction was clearly built up with each component of the building having a specific loadbearing construction. The container-like library departments had a simple concrete skeleton to which glass facades were fitted. Between these building sections vertical cores were set up with stairs, lifts and cylinders for wiring which supported the high peripheral building.

This led to a library landscape that evokes memories of the central linkage of reading rooms in Scharoun's Staatsbibliothek, but here it is more clearly structured in departments with separate transparent spaces to the side of a diagonally open hall with information centre, cafe and catalogue centre within open circles. Even more so than in the Gemäldegalerie, here was a structuralist design in which various functions were laid like grids over each other.

The jury, including Ieoh Ming Pei as chairman, Henning Larsen and Richard Rogers, nominated four designs after which President Mitterand awarded the first prize to the French architect Dominique Perrault.

Central hall of the library

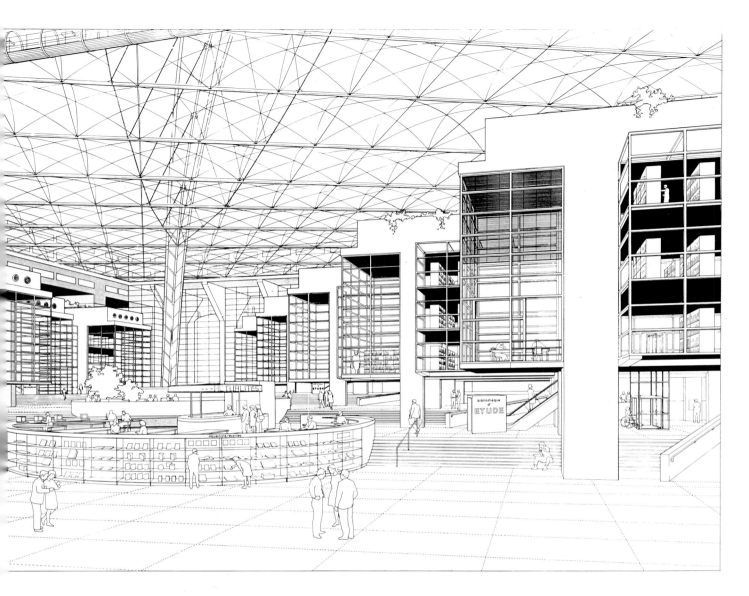

The design shows a clear
construction in different layers

Floor plan of main floor

1 entrance court
2 central hall
3 information centre
4 café
5 catalogues
6 conference room
7 library counter
8 void

bibliothèque d'actualité | *recent acquisitions library*   bibliothèque film et son | *sound and image library*   bibliothèque de recherche | *research library*

bibliothèque enfants | *children's library*   bibliothèque d'étude | *reference library*

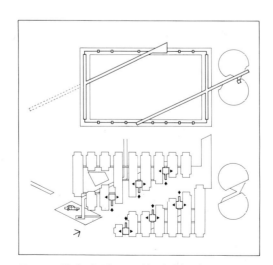

Diagram with the distribution of books (above)
and the transparent container-like building volumes
for various departments and functions

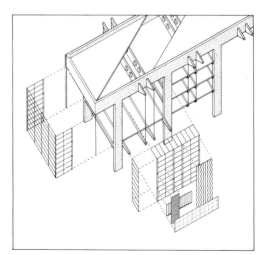

Table construction for the library departments with
possibilities for filling them in

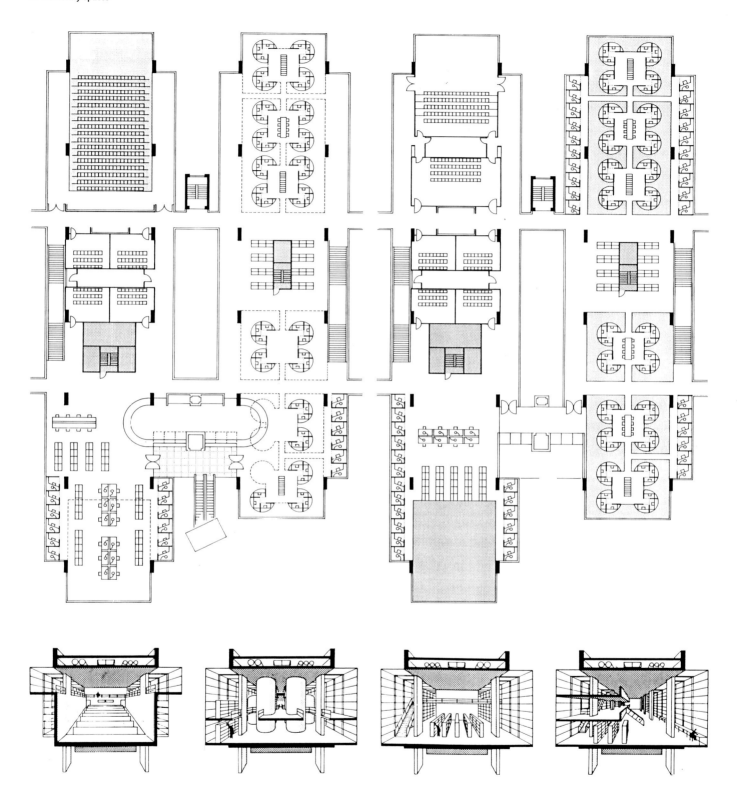

Service building and offices of Estec Noordwijk

Aldo and Hannie van Eyck *Design 1985–1986 Realization 1987–1989*

The European Space Agency and Technology Centre (Estec) in Noordwijk is located against a dune ridge and consists of a collection of industrial buildings. At the end of a comb-shaped building an office block and service building were added. Although both buildings show affinities in use of materials, the differences in function led to divergence in architecture and building volumes.

The office building of two to three floors consists of a configuration of six more or less square 'towers' each of about 16 metres with almost twelve metres between them. They are linked by two intermediate buildings with irregular f oor plans in which the lifts and toilets are found. The towers have square floor plans, which have been smoothed off on the slightly projecting corners. The concrete construction consist of slim columns within the walls and N-shaped porticos around the core. The walls are of timber; on each floor the wall has been built a few centimetres outward. The free manipulation of the basic forms has led to an almost organic architecture. Vertically closed wall segments indicate on the exterior the spot where the columns stand inside.

The service building houses a staff canteen for 550 people, a conference hall, a library and a documentation centre. The floor plan is constructed of a conglomerate of semi-circles with a cross section of 33 metres, with the convex sides fac ng each other. These spaces with varying height surround a patio and a winter garden. What is striking is the way in which the space is structured by the steel construction. Depending on the load, the columns consist of one to eleven tubes with a diameter of eight centimetres. The combined columns have welded base-plates and capping plates. In the main columns are canals for air treatment with an exhaust head and more wiring for lighting, combination equipment and fire-fighting. On the main columns are steel trusses with a flat top and a curved lower edge. For rigidity this lower edge is made of three tubes with loaded partitions. In this way Van Eyck achieved a complex structured spatial form with a relatively simple construction. The walls of the service building also consist of iroko facades, alternated with white wall slabs. The roof edges are finished with copper. The interior acquirec an extra dimension through the use of Van Eyck's favourite colour: the rainbow. For each truss a single colour in a different colour intensity is used, which follows the spectrum of the rainbow in the order of the trusses. Apart from this, yellow is used in the walls and roof zone, around the skylights, as a connection with the daylight.

The Estec buildings at the
edge of the dunes

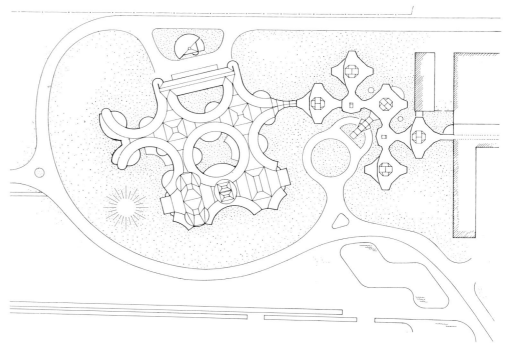

The walls, tilting slightly forward, consist of storey-high iroko facades

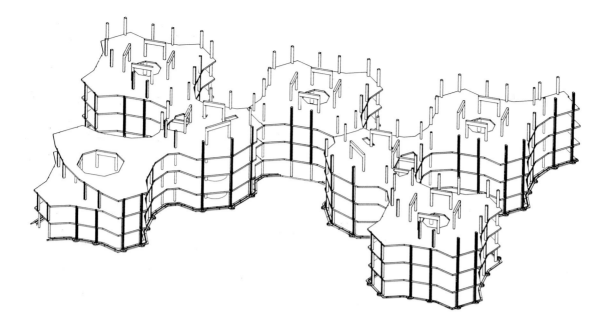

Structural layout of the office building

Detail of a staircase

Floor plan of office building and facilities centre

1	entrance	5	travel office	9 library
2	stairs	6	office	10 winter garden
3	lift	7	restaurant	11 terrace
4	seat	8	conference hall	

Cross sections of restaurant and winter garden

Exterior of
the service
building

Patio with
terrace

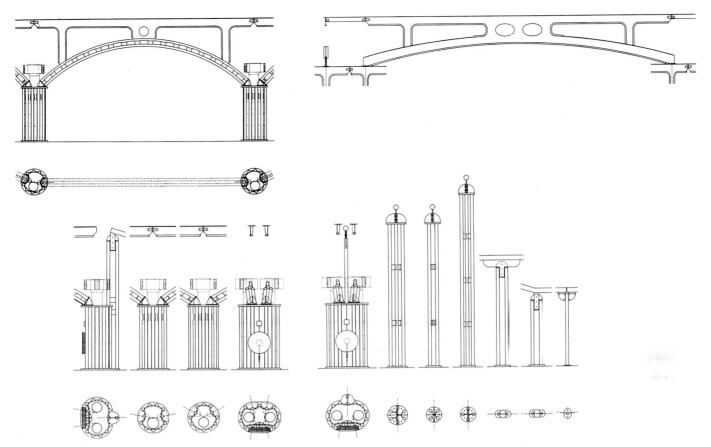

The construction of the loadbearing structure in which wiring and pipes for the air conditioning, electricity ard water are included

Column top with air conditioning

Interior of the restaurant

Ministry of Social Affairs and Employment The Hague

Herman Hertzberger *Design 1979–1984 Realization 1987–1990*

The Ministry for 1800 civil servants is along the Haarlem-Rotterdam railway line opposite the Laan van Nieuw Oost-Indië station on the boundary with Voorburg. It is located between two residential neighbourhoods.

In the first design there were five separate building sections, for the most part in a T-shape or TT-shape, on a continuous inner street; because of imposed economies, the layout became more compact. The original office landscapes with voids made way for mainly single-person workrooms. At this stage the configuration became less clear and the office spaces and the central spaces, which had become smaller, became interwoven in a complex manner.

On the station side, parking is situated under the office building, partly used by travellers who use the train for the rest of their journey. Above this are the general facilities such as restaurant, large conference rooms, library, archives and five office floors. On the western side there are three office floors above the printing works and archives. Here the total building height of five floors links up with the housing opposite; the railway side has seven floors, with the offices being situated so high that users are not looking out at the railway embankment from behind their desks.

For the concrete construction, which is for the most part prefabricated, round columns with a square column top on a two-sided grid of 7.7 metres have been used. This construction grid is rotated thirty five degrees with regard to the longitudinal axis of the building.

The walls are in masonry of almost white concrete blocks with aluminum frames at the office spaces. The secondary stairways are glazed over their total height. The strongly expressive articulation of the office walls is the result of input by the users; originally, Hertzberger intended to keep the receding space as vertical voids within the walls. Because the civil servants were firm in demanding a window directly on the facade, these voids were dropped. On the interior courts which remained, there are mainly conference rooms. The skylights of these courts were also brought a floor lower at the request of the users.

Through the growing need to build in an energy-saving manner, there is little of the loadbearing construction visible in the outer walls. By far the majority of columns are within the walls so that the are no 'cold conductors' in the thermally well-insulated walls.

Aerial photo with the railway station in the foreground. The structural grid is rotated 45 degrees with regard to the longitudinal axis

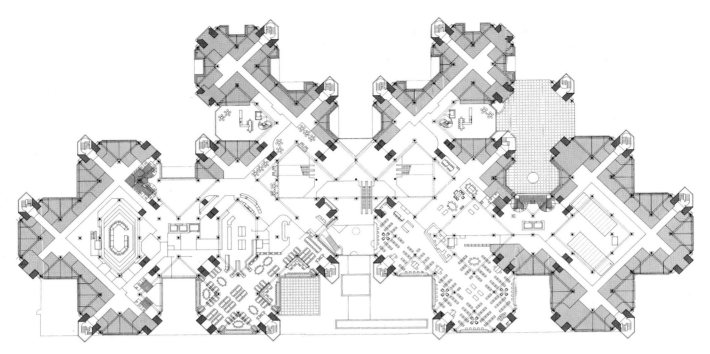

Main floor

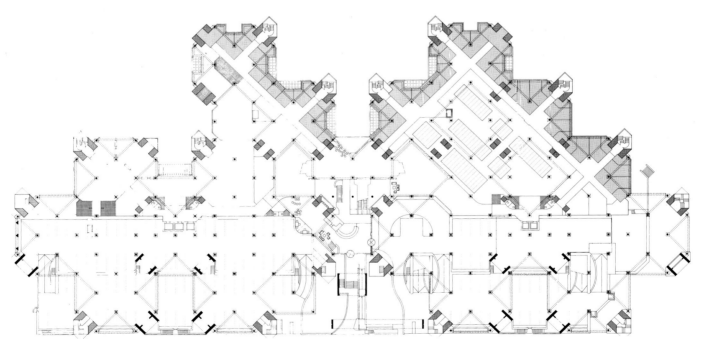

Lower floor

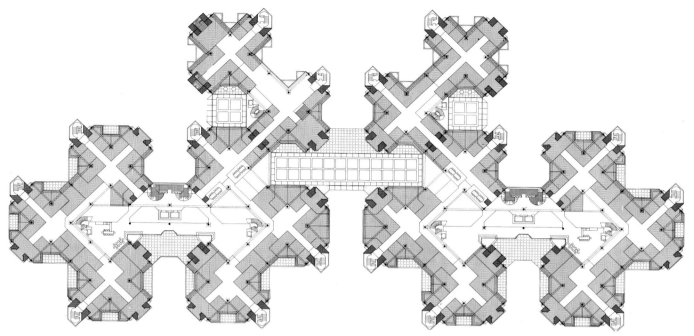

Second floor

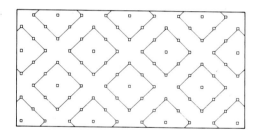

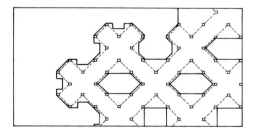

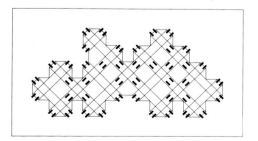

Diagram of basic structure, the diagram of the interpretable zone and the diagram of the wiring shafts

Hall on the main floor

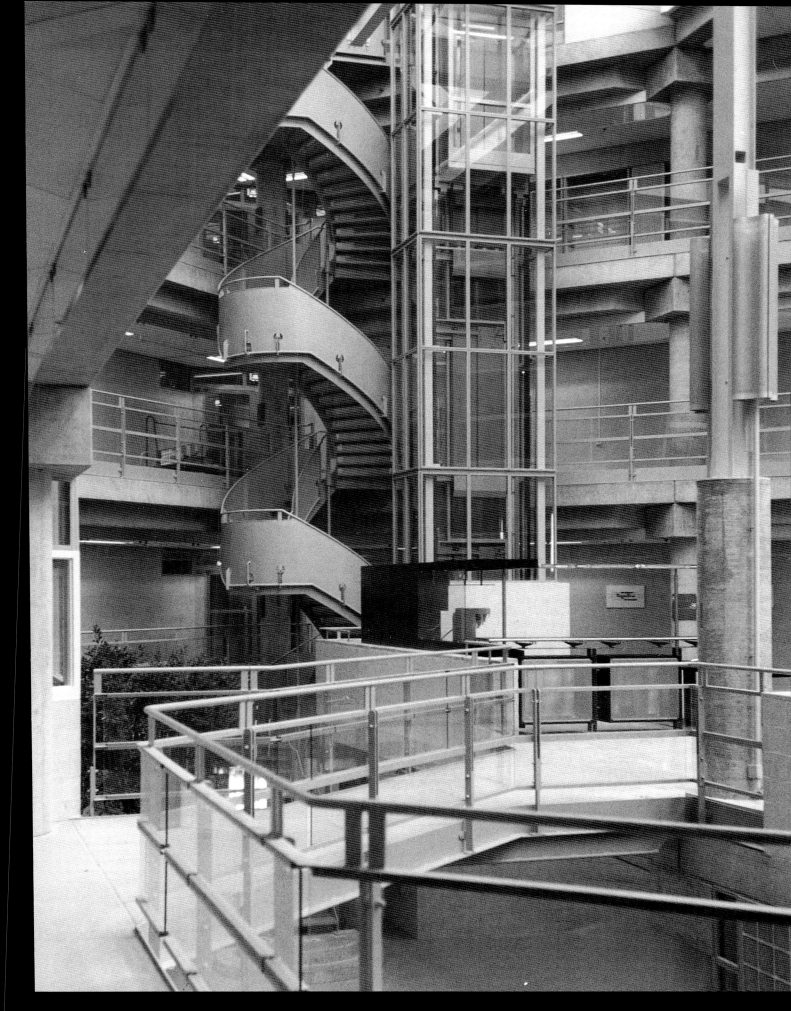

Media-Park Cologne
Herman Hertzberger *Design 1991*

The Media-Park in Cologne is a district with offices, dwellings, studios and secondary functions on a site which has become available on the edge of the inner city. The town planning design by Eberhard Zeidler from Toronto includes among other things six tapering blocks around a centrally located square. For each block, multiple commissions were awarded to three to four architects. For the biggest lot Herman Hertzberger, Jean Nouvel, Rem Koolhaas and Bangert, Jansen, Scholz and Schultes were invited. The jury, led by Gustav Peichl, chose Hertzberger's design which has to be built by 1995.

The total surface area covers about 25,000 m². As well as office space, dwellings and flexible spaces for studios were requested. In the design, Hertzberger was looking for a solution in which the static image of closed blocks would be interrupted. The curved building line on a semi-circular secondary square was the point of departure for five curved office buildings, which are located with the round side facing a raised inner court. The space within these five-storey-high curved office buildings was used to house studios which because of their greater height and free spaces do not fit into the structure of an office building. In the building lines of the site boundaries, galleries are envisaged between two screen-like constructions of columns and beams, to provide access to the big inbuilt elements, which in the future can undergo far-reaching changes because of changing functions. Hertzberger does not want to 'fill' these semi-circular spaces with buildings, but to allow empty spaces around the building volumes. On the upper side it is not planned to have a flat roof slab, the building volumes developed on the basis of their functions can lead to an expressive roofscape. Above the curved strips of offices the dwellings have been designed as the highest building floor.

The design deviates clearly from the surrounding closed blocks with atriums and partly open spaces under skylights. Because of the curves of the blocks, people look into the open inner court 'as if from bays', which is quite strongly narrowed at points. Hertzberger expects that this configuration will arouse the curiosity of passers-by and wants to emphasise the public function through the location of cafés, restaurants, kiosks and so on.

Behind the galleries, which are filled in with various means from glass bricks to closed surfaces, Hertzberger hopes for a pre-eminently structuralist completing of the high, semi-cylindrical spaces with flexible and extendable studio-type spaces with voids as resting spaces between them. Much will depend of the development of the plan and in particular these contents and any later adjustments or extensions.

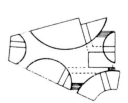

Configuration

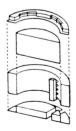

Main structure of the curved buildings

Filling in the blocks in Eberhard Zeidler's urban design, from the top down, Herman Hertzberger, M. Volf, J. Schürmann, Kölner Bucht and Jean Nouvel

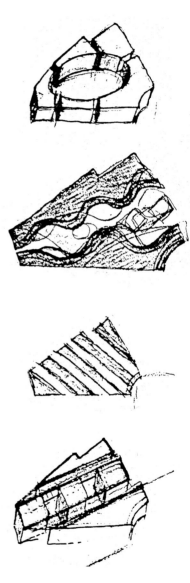

Sketches from the design process

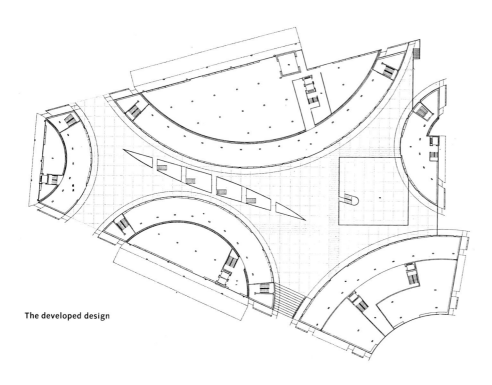

The developed design

Map of the Netherlands

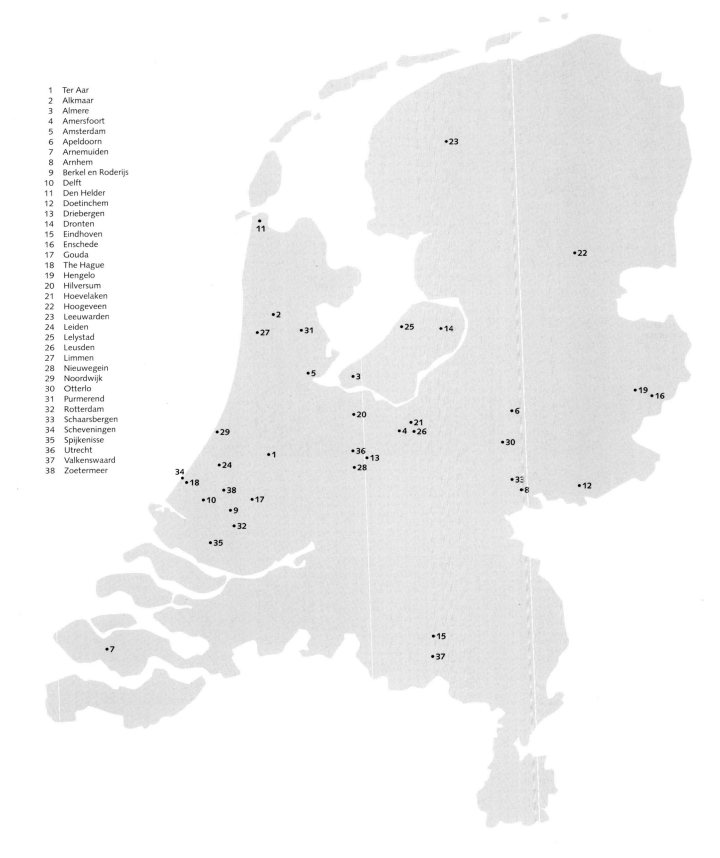

1 Ter Aar
2 Alkmaar
3 Almere
4 Amersfoort
5 Amsterdam
6 Apeldoorn
7 Arnemuiden
8 Arnhem
9 Berkel en Roderijs
10 Delft
11 Den Helder
12 Doetinchem
13 Driebergen
14 Dronten
15 Eindhoven
16 Enschede
17 Gouda
18 The Hague
19 Hengelo
20 Hilversum
21 Hoevelaken
22 Hoogeveen
23 Leeuwarden
24 Leiden
25 Lelystad
26 Leusden
27 Limmen
28 Nieuwegein
29 Noordwijk
30 Otterlo
31 Purmerend
32 Rotterdam
33 Schaarsbergen
34 Scheveningen
35 Spijkenisse
36 Utrecht
37 Valkenswaard
38 Zoetermeer

Place-name index

Index of names

Apon, Dick C. *12, 18, 44, 45, 60, 80*
Archigram *28, 31*
Architectonica *216*
Arp, Jean *76*
Bakema, Jaap *7, 10, 12, 14, 15, 30, 32, 33, 34, 60, 64*
Bangert, Jansen, Scholz & Schultes *234*
Bax, M.F.Th. *34, 35*
Bekaert, Geert *102*
Berg, J.A. van den *102*
Berlage, H.P. *7, 8, 9, 16, 22*
Blom, Piet *18, 19, 24, 25, 26, 28, 30, 38, 64, 68, 72, 106, 126*
Blom van Assendelft, Rob *106*
Bo, Jørgen *40*
Bodegraven, Wim van *14*
Boer, Sake de *26, 27*
Bofill, Ricardo *216*
Bonnema, Abe *44, 45, 150, 196*
Boon, Gert *12, 20, 64, 84, 88, 92, 93, 94*
Boon, J. *206*
Bosch, Theo *28, 29*
Botta, Mario *216*
Brancusi, Constantin *76*
Brinkman, J.A. *10, 11*
Brinkman, M. *12, 14*
Brinkman, Willem *33*
Broek, J.H. van den *15, 30, 32, 33*
Brouwer, H. *64, 80*
Buch, Joseph *44*
Buchanan, Peter *44, 48*
Bijvoet, B. *7, 11, 20, 22*
Cahen, Abel *46*
Campman, H. *174*
Candilis, Georges *10, 38, 40, 41*
Choisy, J.L.C. *80*
Constant *26, 28, 30, 31, 48*
Costa, Mendes da *182*
Davidse, Wim *20, 26, 29, 116, 158*
Dudok, W.M. *8, 10*
Duiker, Jan *7, 10, 11, 16, 20, 22*
Duintjer, M.F. *202*
Dijk, Hans van *44*
Eesteren, Cornelis van *10*
Embden, S.J. van *18, 68, 106*
Ernst, Max *76*
Erskine, Ralph *14*
Eyck, Aldo van *7, 10, 12, 14, 16, 17, 18, 20, 22, 24, 26, 30, 40, 46, 47, 52, 64, 76, 154, 178, 220*
Eyck, Hannie van *46, 47, 52, 220*
Fledderus, Rein H. *102*
Förderer, Walter M. *26*
Frampton, K. *36*
Friedman, Yona *26, 28, 31, 48*
Froger, J.C. *80*
Giacometti, Alberto *76*
Gool, F.J. van *84*
Goor, Martin van *214*
Granpré Molière, M.J. *8*
Greiner, Onno *26, 28, 96, 166, 170*
Grinten, G.J. van der *80*
Gutbrod, Rolf *46, 212*
Gutmann, Rolf *10*
Haan, Herman *18*
Habraken, N.J. *32, 36*
Hardy, Joop *12*
Hendriks *174*
Hepworth, Barbara *76*
Hertzberger, Herman *7, 12, 18, 20,*

21, 22, 23, 24, 26, 27, 34, 36, 38, 40, 44, 46, 47, 48, 64, 80, 84, 85, 86, 87, 88, 92, 95, 112, 116, 144, 182, 212, 216, 228, 234
Heijdenrijk, Leo *20, 21, 24, 26, 27, 28, 29, 34, 35, 38, 84, 88, 89, 90, 91, 92, 95, 102, 140, 162*
Hollein, Hans *14*
Holscher, Knud *40, 41*
Hoogstad, Jan *162*
Howell, William *10*
Istha, D.J. *202*
Jelles, E.J. *64*
Joedicke, Jürgen *16, 46*
Jong, F.M. de *34, 35*
Josic, Alex *38, 41*
Kahn, Louis I. *16, 38, 39*
Kasteel, Bart van *28, 29, 190, 194*
Keyser, Hendrick de *7*
Kjærholm, Hanne *40, 43*
Klerk, Michel de *44*
Klingeren, Frank van *22, 23, 24, 25, 134*
Klunder, Henk *32, 33*
Kölner Bucht *236*
Koolhaas, Rem *46, 216, 234*
Kramer, J.H. *202*
Kranendonk, A. van *80*
Kristinsson, Jón *162*
Krohn, Gunnar *40, 41*
Kropholler, A.J. *8*
Lafour, Lucien *106*
Larsen, Henning *40, 41, 216*
Le Corbusier *12, 22, 23, 38, 39*
Lévi-Strauss, Claude *38*
Löfström, Kaarina *42*
Lüchinger, Arnulf *36, 38*
Lund, Kjell *40, 42*
Maaskant, H.A. *84*
Maki, Fumihiko *216*
Mäkinen, Matti K. *40, 42*
Matthew, Sir Robert H. *84*
Mies van der Rohe, L. *213*
Mol, Jos *26, 27, 28, 29, 32, 34, 35, 140*
Mourik, Dick van *202*
Newman, Oscar *10*
Nouvel, Jean *216, 234, 236*
Olphen, H. van *34, 35*
Parvin, Iraj *26, 27*
Pei, Ieoh Ming *216*
Peichl, Gustav *234*
Perrault, Dominique *216*
Pevsner, Antoine *76*
Prouvé, Jean *40, 41*
Rasmussen, E. Hartvig *40, 41*
Reijenga, Henk *26, 27, 32, 34, 35*
Rhijn, Sier van *102*
Rietveld, Gerrit Th. *8, 9, 16, 64, 76*
Rogers, Richard *216*
Rosdorff, Flip *44, 206*
Ruys, Mien *150, 196*
Safdie, Moshe *14, 15*
Samusamu, Wim *106*
Sanders, Th. *7, 8*
Schader, J. *84*
Scharoun, Hans *212, 213, 216*
Schiedhelm, Manfred *38, 41*
Schindler, Rudolph *14*
Schrofer, Jurriaan *12, 13*
Schröder-Schräder, Truus *8, 9*
Schürmann, J. *236*

Schweighofer, Anton *162, 163*
Sjoer, A. *126*
Skriver, Poul-Erik *40*
Slaatos, Nils *40, 42*
Smithson, Alison & Peter *10, 14*
Smulders, Bert *106*
Steidle, Otto *22, 34, 36, 37*
Stigt, Joop van *18, 19, 20, 24, 25, 28, 29, 40, 44, 60, 64, 72, 100, 190*
Stirling, James *216*
Strauven, Francis *17*
Sijmons, Karel *64, 102*
Tajiri, Shinkichi *76*
Tange, Kenzo *30, 31, 33, 38*
Tennekes, Jan H. *22, 28, 174*
Thies, Rolf Rickard *40, 42, 44*
Thut, Doris & Ralph *34, 36, 37*
Tijen, W. van *18, 68, 106*
Uhl, Ottokar *36. 37*
Utzon, Jørn *40, 43*
Verheul, Jan *29*
Verhoeven, Jan *20, 32, 33, 40, 45, 64, 84, 88, 92. 95*
Visser, G.J. *154*
Vlugt, L.C. van der *10, 11*
Völcker, John *10*
Volf, M. *236*
Wagner, Otto *7*
Weeber, Carel *112*
Weber, Jos *34, 36, 37*
Wiebenga, J.G. *11*
Willegen, T. van *202*
Witstok, Nico *33*
Wohlert, Vilhelm *40*
Woods, Shadrach *10, 38, 41*
Zanstra, Piet *84, 190*
Zeidler, Eberhard *44, 234, 236*
Zocher, Jan D. jr. *7*

Literature

Essay

'Forum – Maandblad voor architectuur en gebonden kunsten' 1959 no 7 to 1963 no 3, and a supplementary number in July 1967, published as 1963 no 4. The total of 23 issues were edited by Dick C. Apon, Aldo van Eyck, Jaap B. Bakema, Gert Boon, Joop Hardy and Herman Hertzberger. Jurriaan Schrofer was responsible for typografic design

Lüchinger, Arnulf: 'Structuralism in Architecture and Urban Planning' (in English, German and French), Stuttgart 1981

Lüchinger, Arnulf: 'Strukturalismus – eine neue Strömung in der Architektur', special issue, Bauen+Wohnen 1976 no 1

Ekholm, Anders, Nils Ahrbom, Peter Broberg, Poul-Erik Skriver: 'Utvecklingen mot Strukturalism i Arkitekturen', Stockholm 1980

Buchanan, Peter: 'Forum Fellowship', special number The Architectural Review 1990 no 1116

Buchanan, Peter: 'Nederlandse architectuur is het spoor bijster; eigen traditie ingeruild voor trendy internationalisme', architectuur/bouwen 1988 no 6/7

Joedicke, Jürgen: 'Architecture im Umbruch' and 'Architekturgeschichte des 20. Jahrhunderts', Stuttgart 1980 and 1990

Frampton, Kenneth: 'Modern architecture and the critical present', Architectural Design Profile, London 1982 no 7/8

Groenendijk, Paul and Piet Vollaard: 'Gids voor moderne architectuur in Nederland – Guide to modern architecture in the Netherlands', Rotterdam 1987

Heuvel, Wim J. van: 'Structuralisme: ordenend raster en meervoudig gebruik van de ruimte', 'Structuralisme als ordenend raster en dubbel grondgebruik: het stedelijk dak', 'Structuralisme: veranderingen en uitbreiding tijdens het wonen', 'Structuralisme: ordenend raster en afwijkingen van de gekozen structuur' and 'Structuralisme: een stadhuis als huis voor de stad'. A series of articles in Polytechnisch Tijdschrift, edition Bouwkunde, wegen- en waterbouw 1981 nos 8 to 12

Heuvel, Wim J. van: 'Het structuralisme in enkele kantoorgebouwen – kanttekeningen bij twee ministeries en het PEN-complex', architectuur/bouwen 1984 no 1

Bax, M.F.Th.: 'Structuur en toeval, architectuur: kunst en wetenschap', Plan 1980 no 11

Klotz, Heinrich: 'Moderne und postmoderne – Architektur der Gegenwart 1960–1980', Braunschweig/Wiesbaden 1987

Projects

Burgerweeshuis, IJsbaanpad/Amstelveenseweg, Amsterdam
Strauven, Francis: 'Het Burgerweeshuis van Aldo van Eyck – een modern monument', Amsterdam 1987
(Strauven, Francis): 'Niet om het even – van en over Aldo van Eyck', Amsterdam s.a. (1986) pp 74–75, 96–97
'Aldo van Eyck – projecten 1948–1961' collected publications by Johan van Beek, Groningen 1981. Including:
– Aldo van Eyck: 'Kindertehuis in Amsterdam', Forum 1960/61 no 6–7 pp 195–235
– Aldo van Eyck: 'Kindertehuis in Amsterdam', Bouwkundig Weekblad 1963 no 2 pp 25–30
Joedicke, Jürgen: 'Architektur im Umbruch – Geschichte Entwicklung Ausblick', Stuttgart 1980 pp 157–158
'Architekturgeschichte des 20. Jahrhunderts', Stuttgart 1990 pp 155–156 (chapter dealing with structuralism is almost identical to 'Architektur im Umbruch' from 1980)
'Bewaar het Weeshuis, Maintain the Orphanage' edited by Herman Hertzberger (action paper), Amsterdam s.a. (1987)

Prix de Rome 1962
'Eindkamp voor de Prix de Rome 1962' design with commentary by architect and jury, Forum 1963 no 1 pp 4–52
Prix de Rome 1962, Bouwkundig Weekblad 1963 no 1 pp 7–22

Chapel for 'Kerk en Wereld', Driebergen
Hezik, V. van a.o.: 'Aantekeningen bij de meervoudige opdracht', Katholiek Bouwblad 1964 no 14 pp 312–325
Special number 'Mededelingen' of the Prof. dr. G. van der Leeuwstichting, Amsterdam 1964 no 27 pp 1163–1211
Beek, Johan van de: 'Aldo van Eyck – projekten 1962–1976', Groningen 1982, pp 1–9; reprint from World Architecture no 3, London 1966 pp 123–129
Nooteboom, Cees: 'Unbuilt Netherlands', New York 1985 pp 82–83 (Translation of the Dutch edition which does not include this design)
(Heuvel, Wim J. van): 'Het ontwerp van Aldo van Eyck', Cobouw 21 May 1964

Temporary student restaurant, Drienerlo, Enschede
Beerends, Arnaud (A.B.): 'Voorlopige mensa', TABK 1969 no 23 pp 564–565
Hiddema, Seerp: 'Piet Blom en de Kunst van het bouwen', Groningen 1984 pp 17–18
Huygen, Peter: 'Vorm geven aan de campus – de architectuur van de Universiteit Twente', Enschede 1990 pp 44–45

Staff canteen University of Twente, Enschede
Beerends, Arnaud V. and Hans Pullens: 'Joop van Stigt – variaties op een thema, Personeelskantine T.H. Twente', TABK 1968 no 3 pp 54–63
Huygen, Peter: 'Vorm geven aan de campus – de architectuur van de Universiteit Twente', Enschede 1990 pp 41, 48–49

Sculpture pavilion for Sonsbeek, Arnhem
Quaerens, Peter: 'Paviljoen Sonsbeek '66', Katholiek Bouwblad 1966 no 18 pp 412–415
Beek, Johan van de: 'Aldo van Eyck – projekten 1962–1976', Groningen 1982 pp 14–22; reprint from World Architecture London 1967 no 4 pp 58–65
(Strauven, Francis): 'Niet om het even – van en over Aldo van Eyck', Amsterdam s.a. (1986) pp 58–59

Town hall Valkenswaard
Vercruysse, A.H. Th. (A.V.): 'Een raadhuis voor Valkenswaard', Katholiek Bouwblad 1967 no 4 and 5 pp 73–91 and 97–120
Lüchinger, Arnulf: 'Herman Hertzberger', The Hague 1987 pp 345

Town hall Amsterdam
Beerends, Arnaud: 'Een structuur voor het raadhuis van Amsterdam', TABK 1969 no 1 pp 13–34
Pennink (P.K.A.): 'Een stadhuis voor Amsterdammers', Forum (extra number) 1969 no 4 pp 1–27
Heuvel, Wim J. van: 'Stadhuisontwerpen voor Amsterdam 1 en 2', Polytechnisch Tijdschrift, edition Bouwkunde, wegen- en waterbouw, 1969 no 17 pp 670–683 and no 18 pp 712–721
Heuvel, Wim J. van: 'Structuralisme: een stadhuis als huis voor de stad', Polytechnisch Tijdschrift, edition Bouwkunde, wegen- en waterbouw, 1981 no 12 pp 638–644

The Zilveren Schor, Zilveren Schorweg 1, Arnemuiden
Buffinga, A.: 'Vrij zijn in Arnemuiden' with note on plan by the architect, Bouw 1968 no 29/30 pp 1082–1091
Greiner, Onno: 'Jeugdcentrum "Het Zilveren Schor" te Arnemuiden', Bouwkundig Weekblad 1967 no 12 pp 197–204
E.H. (Hartsuyker): 'Jugendhaus "Het Zilveren Schor" in Arnemuiden, Holland', Werk 1968 no 2 pp 81–83

Town hall, Middenweg 3a, Limmen
Heuvel, Wim J. van: 'Variaties met vierkanten', Hout 1970 no 2 pp 2–13

Church-building ideas competition, Utrecht – Overvecht
'Resultaten Ideeënprijsvraag Kerkbouw', special numbers TABK 1968 no 19 pp 459–482 and no 24 pp 588–611
Dendermonde, Max: 'Environmental Design', Amersfoort 1974 pp 50–51

De Bastille University of Twente, Enschede
Beerends, Arnaud, Ruud Brouwers and Johan van de Beek: 'Stedebouwkundig plan Drienerlo en nieuwe mensa', TABK 1969 no 23 pp 566–590 and no 25 pp 628–631
Huygen, Peter: 'Vorm geven aan de campus', Enschede 1990 pp 50–60
Woerkom, Dick van and Rob Blom van Assendelft: 'Mensa te Enschede', Plan 1970 no 1 pp 42–56

Diagoon dwellings, Gebbenlaan, Delft – Buitenhof
Lüchinger, Arnulf: 'Herman Hertzberger', The Hague 1987 pp 72–85 and 346
Hertzberger, Herman: 'Ruimte maken, ruimte laten', Delft 1984 pp 72–81
Hertzberger, Herman: 'Lessons for students in architecture', Rotterdam 1991
pp 157–163

Head offices Centraal Beheer, Prins Willem Alexanderlaan 651, Apeldoorn
Lüchinger, Arnulf: 'Herman Hertzberger', The Hague 1987 pp 86–145
'Documentatie bouwtechniek TH Bouwkunde Delft: Kantoorgebouw Centraal
Beheer Apeldoorn' with contributions from H.A. Dicke (construction), J.W.L. Kruyt
and W. van Vonno (engineering) and B.A. Rietmeijer (building methodology), Delft
1971
Reinink, Wessel: 'Herman Hertzberger, architect', Rotterdam 1991 pp 42–51
Heuvel, Wim J. van: 'Hoofdkantoor voor Centraal Beheer in Apeldoorn',
Polytechnisch Tijdschrift, edition Bouwkunde, wegen- en waterbouw, 1970 no 16
pp 647–656
'Centraal Beheer', various writers, Plan 1970 no 5 pp 328–340
Beerends, Arnaud: 'Valkenswaard – Amsterdam – Apeldoorn, de hink-stap-sprong
van Herman Hertzberger', Wonen-TABK 1973 no 5 pp 9–25

From urban roof to Kasbah, Zwavertsweg/Jac Perkstraat, Hengelo
Borssum, Herrie van and Piet Blom: 'Wonen als stedelijk dak', Loenen aan de Vecht
s.a. (around 1966 and later reprints)
Blom, Piet: 'Kasbah Hengelo, toelichting', TABK 1969 no 22 pp 548, 552–560
Heuvel, Wim J. van: 'De Kasbah een werkelijk experiment', Polytechnisch Tijdschrift,
edition Bouwkunde, wegen- en waterbouw, 1975 no 13 pp 417–424
Blom, Piet: 'Experimentele Woningbouw', The Hague 1976 pp 24–25
'Experimentele woningbouw – ontwerpen met predikaat 1971–1972', The Hague
s.a. (1977) pp 20–27
'Woningbouwdocumentatie', The Hague s.a. (1981) pp 6
Rigo, stichting: 'Projectonderzoek Kasbah', Amsterdam 1978
Instituut voor Toegepaste Sociologie: 'Bewonersonderzoek Kasbah', Nijmegen 1977

Multi-functional community centre 't Karregat, Broekakkerseweg, Eindhoven
'Documentatie bouwtechniek TH Bouwkunde Delft: Wijkcentrum 't Karregat Eind-
hoven' with contributions from Gert Jonker (interview Van Klingeren), C.J. van Zwet
(supervision), L. Wagenmans (construction), C.W. van Dorsser and J. Roos (acous-
tics) and J.J. Jonkman (installations), Delft 1974
Jonker, Gert, Van Klingeren, C.J. van Zwet: ''t Karregat', Bouw 1973 no 52
pp 1581–1584
Zwinkels, Cees: ''t Karregat is nog maar half open na grondige verbouwing', De
Architect 1981 no 5 pp 50–59
Boer, Hubert de and Edzard Luursema: ''t Karregat op weg naar het isolement',
Wonen-TABK 1974 no 7 pp 23–28

Applied Mathematics and Computer Centre, Enschede
Dendermonde, Max: 'Environmental Design', Amersfoort 1974 pp 64–67
Huygen, Peter: 'Vorm geven aan de campus – de architectuur van de Universiteit
Twente', Enschede 1990 pp 25–28

Nursing home De Drie Hoven, Louis Chrispijnstraat 50, Amsterdam
Lüchinger, Arnulf: 'Herman Hertzberger', The Hague 1987 pp 150–183
Hertzberger, Herman: 'Verzorgingscomplex voor bejaarden in Amsterdam', Bouw
1976 no 12 and 'Architectuur uit Bouw' 1976 pp 49–54
Stuvel, H.J.: 'Wooncomplex De drie hoven, Amsterdam/Slotervaart', Rijswijk 1975
pp 1–12 (brochure HBG)

Social Services and dwellings, Noordvliet 37, Leeuwarden
Bonnema A.: 'Kantoorgebouw met woningen te Leeuwarden', Bouw 1976 no 22
pp 53–60 and 'Architectuur uit Bouw 1976', Rotterdam 1977 pp 202–205
Arthur Drexler: 'Transformations in Modern Architecture', New York 1979 pp 138
Arthur Drexler: 'Transformationen in der modernen Architektur', Düsseldorf 1984
pp 138

Detached house, Retie, Belgium
Heuvel, Wim J. van: 'Een conglomeraat van sferen', De Architect 1977 no 11
pp 65–69
'Aldo van Eyck – Enquête d'une labyrinthienne – In Search of Labyrinthian Clarity –
Maison G.J. Visser, Belgique', l'Architecture d'Aujourd'hui 1975 no 177 pp 26–27
(Strauven, Francis): 'Niet om het even – van en over Aldo van Eyck', Amsterdam s.a.
(1986) pp 124

Library, Raadhuisstraat 25 , Doetinchem
Heuvel, Wim J. van: 'Nieuwe bibliotheek te Doetinchem: voorbeeldige betonarchi-
tectuur', Polytechnisch Tijdschrift, edition Bouwkunde, wegen- en waterbouw, 1976
no 6 pp 345–354
Davidse, W.: 'Bibiotheek in Doetinchem/Holland', Detail 1977 no 1 pp 29–32
Heuvel, Wim J. van: 'Davidse in Doetinchem', De Architect 1976 no 5

Town hall Lelystad
Heijdenrijk, Leo: 'Stadhuis Lelystad', commentary on the competition design,
Amersfoort 1977
Heuvel, Wim J. van: 'Drie stadhuisontwerpen voor Lelystad', Cobouw 29-4-1977

Cultural centre De Flint, Coninckstraat 60, Amersfoort
Greiner, Onno: 'Ontmoetingscentrum te Amersfoort', Bouw 1978 no 8 and 'Archi-
tectuur uit Bouw 1978', Rotterdam 1979 pp 133–138
'Documentatie bouwtechniek TH Bouwkunde Delft: 'Cultureel centrum De Flint te
Amersfoort' with contributions from Onno Greiner, Martien van Goor, J. Buisman
a.o., Delft 1978
Marck, Marc van der: 'Onno Greiner, architect', Amsterdam 1985 pp 69–71
Steemers, Theo: 'Speelstadje contra cultuurpaleis', Wonen-TABK 1975 no 10
pp 5–14
Greiner, Onno: 'Een speelstadje', Plan 1971 no 8 pp 32–34

Stadthalle, Cigelbergstrasse, Biberach an der Riss, Germany
Marck, Marc van der: 'Onno Greiner, architect', Amsterdam 1985 pp 72–75
Niesten, Joop: 'Stadthalle Biberach: Export van ervaring met ontmoetingscentra',
De Architect 1980 no 9 pp 70–75

College, Brasserskade 1, Delft
Heuvel, Wim J. van: 'Lerarenopleiding in Delft een complex als een gebouwde struc-
tuur', Polytechnisch Tijdschrift, edition Bouwkunde, wegen- en waterbouw, 1978
no 5 pp 247–255
Tennekes, H. Jan: 'Het ontwerpproces in de architectuur', unpublished manuscript,
Gouda 1987

Hubertushuis, Plantage Middenlaan 33, Amsterdam
Hertzberger, Herman, Addie van Roijen-Wordtmann and Francis Strauven: 'Aldo van
Eyck', Amsterdam 1982
Strauven, Francis: 'De stedelijke vervoeging van moderne architectuur – plaats voor
wederkerigheid', Wonen-TABK 1980 no 3 pp 11–30
(Strauven, Francis): 'Niet om het even – van en over Aldo van Eyck', Amsterdam s.a.
(1986) pp 138

Muziekcentrum Vredenburg, Vredenburg, Utrecht
'Muziekcentrum Vredenburg' edited by Wim J. van Heuvel, The Hague 1979.
Offprint Polytechnisch Tijdschrift, edition Bouwkunde, wegen- en waterbouw 1979
no 7 pp 390–476
'Documentatie bouwtechniek TH Bouwkunde Delft: Muziekcentrum Vredenburg'
with contributions from building team members, Delft 1980
Lüchinger, Arnulf: 'Herman Hertzberger', The Hague 1987 pp 184–239
'Muziekcentrum Vredenburg', special number Wonen-TABK 1979 no 24 with com-
mentary by Herman Hertzberger and description by Rob Dettingmeijer

Faculty buildings and library University, Witte Singel, Leiden
Cate, Gerda ten, and Chris Rehorst: 'Ontwerpers over het Leidse universiteitscom-
plex: small was beautiful' with plan commentaries by Bart van Kasteel and Joop van
Stigt, Bouw 1984 no 24 pp 35–53
Mooij, D., Joop van Stigt, Bart van Kasteel and H.W. Bennink: 'Nieuwbouw Rijksuni-
versiteit Leiden', Cement 1981 no 12 pp 765–784

PEN offices, Voltastraat 2, Alkmaar
Cate, Gerda ten: 'De paradox van neutraliteit in en door opmerkelijkheid', with
commentary by the architect, Bouw 1983 pp 53–60
Bonnema, A.: 'Het PEN-bedrijfskantoor in Alkmaar', architectuur/bouwen 1984
pp 25–28
'Hoe bouwt men een witte Olifant', edited by Twijnstra Gudde, Deventer 1983
Bonnema, A.: 'Provincial Electric Company', Architecture and Urbanism 1983 no 10
pp 47–54
Watson, Eric: 'Verwaltungs und Werkstattgebäude der Elektrizitäts-Gesellschaft PEN
in Alkmaar', Deutsche Bauzeitung (db) 1984 no 5 pp 34–37

Academic Medical Centre, Meibergdreef 9, Amsterdam-Southeast
Cox, D.H. 'Het Academisch Medisch Centrum – de eerste uit een reeks van
academische ziekenhuizen', architectuur/bouwen 1986 no 11 pp 11–23
Heuvel, Wim J. van: 'Een "Cité Médicale" aan de rand van de Bijlmer – het AMC
tussen andere academische ziekenhuizen', architectuur/bouwen 1986 no 11
pp 37–47
'Academisch Medisch Centrum bij de universiteit van Amsterdam' edited by
D.H. Cox, The Hague s.a.

Ministry of Education and Science, Europaweg 4, Zoetermeer
Rosdorff architectural bureau: 'De nieuwbouw van het Ministerie van Onderwijs en
Wetenschappen in Zoetermeer', The Hague s.a. (1984)
'Het Ministerie van Onderwijs en Wetenschappen in Zoetermeer', architectuur/
bouwen 1984 no 1 pp 15–23
'Ministerie van Onderwijs en Wetenschappen te Zoetermeer', Bouw 1985 no 19
pp 25–30

Bibliothèque de France, Paris
Buchanan, Peter: 'Forum Fellowship', Architectural Review 1990 no 1116 pp 65–69
Reinink, Wessel: 'Herman Hertzberger, architect', Rotterdam 1991 pp 102–107
(Maas, Tom): 'Bibliothèque de France', architectuur/bouwen 1989 no 9 pp 8–9

Service building and offices of Estec, Keplerlaan 1, Noordwijk
Buchanan, Peter: 'Forum Fellowship: Architect Ludens Aldo en Hanny van Eyck',
Architectural Review 1990 no 1116 pp 35, 41–57
Heuvel, Wim J. van: 'Formes, textures, couleurs – extension de l'Estec, Pays-Bas',
Techniques & Architecture 1990 no 386 pp 99–105
Dijk, Hans van: 'Laagbouw op hoog niveau', Jaarboek/Yearbook 1989–1990
Architectuur in Nederland/Architecture in the Netherlands pp 50–52 and 55–57

Ministry of Social Affairs and Employment, Anna van Hannoverstraat 4, The Hague
Lüchinger, Arnulf: 'Herman Hertzberger', The Hague 1987 pp 366–367
Herman Hertzberger and Tom Maas: 'Ministerie SZW: eenheid in verscheidenheid',
architectuur/bouwen 1991 no 1 pp 18–28
Peter Buchanan: 'Beheer's big brother', Architectural Review 1991 no 1129 pp 28–39
Jan Rutten: 'Ministerie van Sociale Zaken en Werkgelegenheid', Rotterdam/The
Hague 1991
'Ministerie van SZW', Projectanalyse 1991 no 6, special number

Sources of illustrations